THE SCREAM

On the third night, the twenty-eighth, two in the morning brought forth screams that made Corey pull a pillow over her head. They were the cries of a child in absolute terror.

Tom dashed downstairs and headed to the kitchen. As he snapped on the kitchen light, the smoke alarm wailed and, as quickly, went silent. The scream was still there and Tom approached the door to the mudroom. Corey had come downstairs a minute or so behind him. As he reached for the doorknob he could almost feel the child scream. The sound was deafening.

Tom grabbed the doorknob and just as suddenly let go.

"It's hot!" he yelled.

"Don't touch it again. There might be a fire in the mudroom," Corey warned. Tom didn't listen. He braced himself against the door and again reached for the knob. He quickly turned it and eased the door open.

The knob was now cool. The screaming stopped. The mudroom was empty...

The Uninvited

True Tales of the Unknown, Vol. II

Edited by Sharon Jarvis

BANTAM BOOKS
NEW YORK • TORONTO • LONDON • SYDNEY • AUCKLAND

THE UNINVITED
TRUE TALES OF THE UNKNOWN, VOLUME II
A Bantam Book / November 1989

ISBN 0-553-28251-4

Published simultaneously in the United States and Canada

Bantam Books are published by Bantam Books, a division of
Bantam Doubleday Dell Publishing Group, Inc. Its trademark,
consisting of the words "Bantam Books" and the portrayal of a
rooster, is Registered in U.S. Patent and Trademark Office and
in other countries. Marca Registrada. Bantam Books, 666 Fifth
Avenue, New York, New York 10103.

PRINTED IN THE UNITED STATES OF AMERICA

KR   0 9 8 7 6 5 4 3 2 1

*For my father, who always
enjoyed a good story.*

Contents

Acknowledgments

Without the help of the following people, this book would not be possible: Mary Ann Bramstrup, Jim Knusch, Lee Svensson, Anne Pinzow, Stephen Kaplan, Roxanne Salch Kaplan, Bob Stone, Maurice Schwalm, Joel Martin, George Anderson, Dale Kaczmarek, Michael A. Frizzell, Lee Chapman, Chris Martin, Elise Martin, Stan Gordon, Dr. Berthold Schwarz, Countess Misty, Gene Snyder, Joseph Sena, Pearl Gonzalez, Norman Basile, Patrick and Josette Garrison, Carolina, John Krysko, Bill Clark, Hillyer Senning, and Jane White of the Baltimore Convention & Visitors Assn.

When writing to any of the following people and/or organizations, please include a self-addressed, stamped envelope.

Stephen Kaplan
The Parapsychology Institute of America
or The Vampire Research Center
P.O. Box 252
Elmhurst, NY 11373

Joel Martin, George Anderson
P.O. Box 5442
Babylon, NY 11707

Carolina
Long Island, NY
1-516-884-1456

Baltimore Area Convention & Visitors Assn.
1 East Pratt Street, Plaza Level
Baltimore, MD 21202
1-800-282-6632

Michael A. Frizzell
The Enigma Project
P. O. Box 462
Reistertown, MD
  21136

Dale Kaczmarek
Ghost Research Society
P. O. Box 205
Oak Lawn, IL 60454

Countess Misty
c/o Vampire's Journal
P. O. Box 5686
Stockton, CA 95205

Raymond D. Manners
International Fortean
  Organization
P. O. Box 367
Arlington, VA 22210

Lee Chapman
American Astrology
  Magazine
475 Park Avenue South
New York, NY 10016

Gene Snyder,
  Literature Team
Brookdale Community
  College
Lincroft, NJ 07738

Stan Gordon
Pennsylvania
  Association for the
  Study of the
  Unexplained (PASU)
6 Oakhill Avenue
Greensburg, PA 15601

The PASU UFO
  24-hour hotline:
  412-838-7768

Dr. Berthold E.
  Schwarz
P. O. Box 4030
Vero Beach, FL 32964

Joseph Sena,
  Sena Graphics
P. O. Box 625
FDR Station
New York, NY 10150

Bill Clark
P. O. Box 361762
Melbourne, FL
  32936-1762

Robert Stone
America's Stonehenge
  at Mystery Hill
29 Highland Avenue
Derry, NH 03038

Maurice Schwalm
P. O. Box 3522
Kansas City, KS
  66103-0522

For information about
Dark Shadows
conventions,
contact:
Dark Shadows Festival
P. O. Box 92
Maplewood, NJ 07040

Introduction

Is it possible that a great many people, more than ever imagined, have seen or talked to a ghost?

In 1987, Epcot Center—the famous educational and entertainment center in Florida—took a poll of attendees. Thirteen percent—an apt number—said they'd seen a ghost. Thirty-three percent believed in ghosts. A national survey by a research center of the University of Chicago found that 42 percent of the people polled had been in contact with someone who died. Among those who had lost a spouse, the rate of contact rose to almost two-thirds.

Ask friends or relatives if something unusual—or strange—has ever happened to them. Ask if their house is haunted or they've ever had psychic visions. The answers will astonish and frighten you. Because there isn't anyone who doesn't have an Aunt Emma who reads cards and tells the future or who doesn't have a funny spot in his house where he'd rather not stand.

In the first *True Tales of the Unknown*, after years of being fascinated with such stories, I searched for and found seven genuine tales of the supernatural. These tales came from old reference books, clippings from newspaper "morgues," actual tape recordings made by psychic investigators, and attested-to manuscripts written by the people who actually experienced their own step into the beyond.

All the stories in this new collection are also true. They really happened. What you are reading will, in many instances, be the actual words spoken. All the stories were originally written by the people who researched them—or who lived them—and then were edited. You are reading the facts, incredible facts in every terrifying detail, as they happened.

Many of the researchers who contributed to the first volume of *True Tales* are again represented here, especially Stephen Kaplan, radio and television host Joel Martin, and psychic George Anderson. Many new contributors I first met as a member of the International Fortean Organization, which is dedicated to chronicling bizarre events. INFO has led to a broadening of my national network of psychic and supernatural investigators, such as Dale Kaczmarek of the Ghost Research Society, Michael Frizzell of the Enigma Project, and Stan Gordon of PASU. These dedicated people continue to look for answers to age-old questions, even though the answers, or merely the search for those answers, only raise *more* questions. . . .

What is important to remember is that, if the polls are correct, more and more people realize that "something" is happening out there. There are more things in heaven and earth, dear reader, than you ever dreamt of. And these stories are proof. Join us, if you dare, and read the true tales of: the ghost lights of North Carolina, the most haunted cemetery in Chicago, the ancient sacrificial altar in New Hampshire, the poltergeist that hated religion, the wonderworker of the Santa Fe Trail, and much, much more. . . .

And, unless noted otherwise, every name, place, date, and event are absolutely and most assuredly true!

Sharon Jarvis
Staten Island, New York

Eye of the Assassin

This is the intensely personal story of a young woman who thought she was losing her mind; it was provided by Lee Chapman, editor of American Astrology Magazine.

For years, Pat Charters (not her real name) suffered severe depressions and mental aberrations. She had two near-breakdowns, one in 1963, the other in 1968.

It wasn't until years later that she discovered these incidents were psychically connected to her, to each other, to two separate killings—and to the assassins involved. This is a chilling true story, with a twist.

"Mom, I don't feel good," said the sad-eyed teenage girl. Wearing a flannel nightgown, she stood barefoot in the middle of the kitchen. It was the morning of November 22, 1963, and the kitchen was in the modest home of the Charters family of Salina, Kansas.

Glancing at the plastic clock over the sink, her mother sighed deeply. "It's after eight o'clock, and here you are not dressed and telling me you don't feel good. Obviously you're not going to school." Dorothy Charters snapped around to the stove to finish measuring out the coffee, took a moment to compose herself, and then said in a calmer, more concerned voice, "Well, what's wrong?"

"I don't know . . . I just don't feel good," Pat Charters said in a low, defeated voice. Something was wrong but she couldn't explain it.

Her mother, still with her back to Pat, said, "Can't you be a little more specific?"

At this, Pat broke into a loud fit of crying that sent shivers up Dorothy's spine. She spun around to see her daughter sitting hunched over the kitchen table, head in arms, shoulders shaking violently with the force of her sobs.

"What is it, honey? What on earth is wrong?" she asked, clasping her daughter in her arms.

"I don't know, but I can't go out there today. I just can't!" Pat blurted between gasps for breath and noisy sobs.

It's just the usual nonsense, her mother decided, and loosened her hug ever so slightly. She'd been through this kind of thing before but had never been able to come up with a reasonable way of dealing with it. She couldn't very well physically dress Pat, throw her over her shoulder, and carry her out to the bus stop. The girl was seventeen years old and already an inch taller than Dorothy.

Her voice took on a stricter, though not unkind tone. "Is there some reason why you don't want to go to school today? Your homework, a test today, a boyfriend?"

"It doesn't have anything to do with school! I don't know what's wrong! I just can't face going out there today, that's all! Can't I just stay here with you? I think I'd feel better if I could just be with you for a while."

She looked, Dorothy couldn't help thinking, exactly like a rain-bedraggled kitten perched hopefully on the doorstep waiting to be offered a bowl of sweet milk.

2

"Well," Dorothy said, removing the wildly percolating coffeepot from the burner, "you're already late for school, so that pretty much settles it."

Pat got up from the table. "I'm just going to lie down for a while, okay?"

"All right," her mother answered, already busying herself with the breakfast dishes from her two boys' earlier cereal fest. Her younger son was a rambunctious fourteen, and the elder was a freshman at a local college. While they'd certainly given Dorothy and her husband plenty of headaches, they were the normal boys-will-be-boys variety. But Pat—a moody, insecure, and overly sensitive child—had worried her deeply. Though Dorothy was no psychologist, she suspected the girl might have a serious emotional problem. For the past year or so Pat had seemed unusually depressed, but Dorothy kept hoping that her daughter was merely going through a particularly difficult and drawn-out adolescence and that one of these days she'd snap out of it . . . perhaps by the time Dorothy finished the dishes.

In her room at the end of the long hallway, Pat lay curled up on her bed, blankets bunched around her. She felt a little better already, knowing she wouldn't have to see anyone today. But it wasn't enough to stop the trembling she felt deep in her bones.

Pat knew the feeling was just plain old fear. And in this case, because she knew there was no reason for her to be afraid, no reason at all that she could see, its intensity terrified her. As a tear fell onto her pillow, she hoped the awful shaking would pass.

By lunchtime the two of them were watching television, Dorothy in her armchair and Pat sprawled on the carpet a few feet from the television screen. Flickering across the black-and-white screen were the main characters in one of Dorothy's soaps; Nancy

Hughes was bemoaning some family problem to Grandpa Hughes on *As the World Turns*.

Suddenly their familiar images were replaced by a sign: CBS NEWS BULLETIN. Walter Cronkite's voice, shaken and tense, told America that President Kennedy had been shot in Dallas.

Pat's heart thumped violently at the words; all the vagueness of her early-morning fears gathered into a solid lump of shock. Her next, inexplicable reaction was to flush deeply red with shame and guilt, as if she'd been caught with her hand in the cookie jar. Years later she would suspect that her reaction's source was a small, confused, and terrified man cowering in a movie house in Dallas, Texas—a complete stranger whose psychic path she had innocently crossed on a late-November day.

After the assassination, the deep fearfulness Pat had experienced began to wane, but the heavy veil of depression that accompanied it did not. It followed her around like a bad dream she couldn't get out of her mind. But since the depression had been present before the assassination, Pat did not see that the two could have anything to do with each other. And that's why, when she was finally taken to a psychiatrist in 1964, he pronounced her ill enough to be hospitalized. She never mentioned—nor was she asked—that things had gotten much worse on November 22 . . . and had stayed bad for some months afterward.

Her six-week stay in the state mental hospital did not produce an explanation for Pat's severe depression, and she was released to her parents to seek outpatient care until she was "feeling better." No one suggested that she be treated for what is now known as clinical depression, so a scattered course of psychoanalytic sessions was recommended and accepted. The result, after a year of weekly sessions with a very nice little man in a brown suit, was that neither Pat nor the nice little man ever figured out what was wrong with her. The sessions ended by mutual agreement.

Pat continued to experience occasional bouts of unexplainable depression and fits of sudden fearfulness. But it would be years before she would realize that they had nothing to do with her.

The year and a half following Pat's hospitalization had been rough, to put it mildly. Though her high-school teachers had been relatively gentle with her after her return to school, her fellow students had been just short of vicious. There were many rumors about her mysterious disappearance. The result was that Pat was deeply hurt and withdrew into her interest in art.

Pat's academic performance had always been erratic, but she'd known for a long time that she wanted to be an artist of some kind—a painter or perhaps a writer. And she'd been a secret poet. She'd written reams of poetry and kept it all in a black plastic folder that went everywhere with her. When her English teacher discovered this, and convinced Pat to let her see some of them, the door to a whole new world began to crack open.

"Pat, some of the other students and I hold little poetry readings at my house once a week. I'd really like it if you'd come this Wednesday," said Miss Janzen one day just after class.

Pat blushed, shuffled her feet, and allowed the teacher to talk her into attending. So it was at that first poetry gathering at Miss Janzen's that Pat and Lily Merlino spoke to each other for the first time. Oh, they'd seen each other around for years, had gone to the same junior high school even. But they had always been members of separate circles: Lily the unofficial president of the smarty-pants club and Pat the undisputed queen of the beatnik set.

After the poetry readings the small group gathered around Miss Janzen's little dinette table to have tea and cookies and socialize, something Pat wasn't very good at. But then Lily made a clever comment and Pat made an even cleverer one. It was at this precise point that each girl knew she'd not only met her match but also made a lifelong friend.

In 1965 both girls applied to attend the University of Kansas in Lawrence. Miraculously, Pat was accepted, and the girls were stunned when they found they'd be sharing a room—stunned and unbelievably relieved. They spent their first day of orientation giggling over the dorm rules and resolving to break every one as quickly as possible.

Their friendship deepened and they did a lot of things together, including falling in love with two guys who happened to be roommates. But their expected long-term career as co-conspirators was cut short when, just after the second semester rolled around, Pat moved to San Francisco to be with her parents, who had relocated from Kansas, and to go to the Art Institute there.

They planned a dignified and reserved good-bye, but both young women dissolved into childish tears and hugged each other for the first and—they thought—last time. Pat did not return to Lawrence for several years. When she did return, Lily was now married to David, her first love; Pat had also married, but rashly.

On the morning of June 4, 1968, that old feeling of dread hit Pat shortly after she woke up. She got out of bed, got dressed, and tiptoed out of the second-floor apartment she shared with her husband, John. She didn't want to have an argument with him about where she was going (the liquor store), and especially about why she had been neglecting him so severely lately.

6

She'd already told John she preferred to go alone to Lily's party tonight.

They'd been married only a few months, but Pat had known the marriage was a serious mistake even before they got to the altar in the quaint little chapel on the University of Kansas campus. It was clear from the start that he loved her, but she didn't love him—not the way a wife should love a husband.

So she headed downtown to the little liquor store next to the movie theater. Even though Kansas had rather restrictive liquor laws, the liquor store opened at nine A.M. on weekdays. She wanted to get there when they opened, just as she had so many times before. Although she was twenty-one now, Pat looked fifteen—too young to drink. But by now the owner knew her by name and it made Pat feel important to have him reach for her favorite brand of wine and have it in the bag even before she got all the way inside the store.

Afterward she walked down the main street, drinking as she went, until she reached the bridge over the Kaw River around ten A.M. Though she had managed to distract herself from the weird, awful feeling until now, it came back with a vengeance. Her heart thumped, her blood raced, and her breath was short. She felt as if she were having a heart attack.

She settled into a position on the bridge's concrete railing and reached for a cigarette, trying to control the unreasonable fear that threatened to overwhelm her. It suddenly occurred to Pat that she had no idea what year it was. Why she should be wondering about that in the first place, she couldn't guess—but that she did not even know the year came as a crashing shock.

As she took another drink of wine, a thought popped into her confused mind: *It's 1963*.

This so startled her that she dropped her half-smoked cigarette into the river and stared idiotically after it. Perhaps her scrambled brains were a result of the early-morning wine and summer heat. But her heart continued to pump wildly and it felt as if her very soul trembled.

She took another swig and then almost choked when she caught sight of a Lawrence police officer walking slowly in her direction. She hopped down from the railing, shifting the bottle to where she hoped it was hidden, and smiled.

"It's dangerous to be sitting on the bridge like that," he said. "You could fall in." He moved closer to her, but ever so slowly.

Suddenly Pat understood why he was acting so politely. He thought she had been contemplating leaping off the bridge!

"I'm perfectly all right," she assured him, although she wasn't.

"Glad to hear that," he said, falling into step beside her as she moved toward the Lawrence side of the bridge. At the end of the bridge, the patrol car was parked to one side. He moved toward it and raised his hand in a friendly wave. Pat waved back and watched the patrol car cruise down the street and around a bend.

Standing there, she realized she was sorry to see it go. It had been embarrassing but also had proved a distraction from the weird discomfort she'd been feeling—and still felt. Her heart continued to thump wildly.

Why didn't I ask him what year it is? Pat thought to herself. She considered taking a casual stroll through a hardware store or slipping into the local café—likely places for calendars hanging on the wall. But she was afraid. Instead she decided to head over to the northside park, the one with the old train engine in it. Maybe the fog would clear and she would remember the year herself.

Making her way slowly, under the sizzling noonday sun, Pat remembered suddenly and delightedly that she'd been invited to Lily's house for dinner tonight. Lily and her husband, David, had just moved and were having a small housewarming party.

When she reached the park, her wine bottle was almost empty and her feet were killing her. She sat down in the grass and removed her boots. Then, tucking them under an arm, she sat on one of the picnic tables surrounding the antique train and lit another cigarette.

Whispered phrases floated to the surface of her consciousness: *What year is it? What's wrong? What year is it? It's 1963. Something's wrong, wrong, wrong. . . .*

And then—six. The number six. She tossed away the cigarette, set down the bottle, and stared at her hands. Dumbly she watched as her hands slowly turned palms up, automatically and without her conscious permission, and moved closer to her face. Four fingers on her one hand folded down, the other six remained extended. They seemed frozen into this position and they hung like a sign before her eyes.

She stared blankly for a moment before she realized what she was expected to do: count the fingers. One, two, three, four, five, six . . . Six was enough. She didn't know why, only there was no doubt about it.

Pat gazed fixedly at her hands for several minutes before the spell was broken. She shook her head and looked dazedly at the world around her. Despite the heat, she shivered violently.

Absently she gulped down the last of the wine. Then she pulled her boots on over blistered feet and—though it was now only two o'clock in the afternoon—shuffled off to buy more cigarettes and wine. Pat should have been fairly drunk by now. But instead of feeling loose and relaxed, she had the feeling that the world was coming to an end. It was the same feeling she had had years before.

She walked into the nearest liquor store and made her purchase. Opening the heavy glass door to leave, she hesitated, turned, and nearly asked the cashier what year it was. But she felt too foolish and left.

Once outside, Pat removed her boots again. She decided to slowly walk barefoot to Lily's house, about a mile farther up the street. Even so, she knew she would be arriving awfully early—the invitation was for seven P.M.—but she didn't have anywhere else to go.

She concentrated on putting one bare foot in front of the other while the whisperings from the dark side of her mind continued to prick and prod. *What year is it? It's 1963. What does the number six mean?* And the nameless, shapeless sense of fear took on fuller dimensions of hopelessness and horror.

When she finally spotted Lily's house, half a block away, Pat stopped to try to collect herself. She sat down on the curb and took deep breaths. Although she and Lily had been friends for years, Lily had a low tolerance for Pat's "weirdnesses," as she called them. Pat's periodic depressions, her psychic hunches that came true—these things frightened Lily.

Gingerly Pat pulled on her boots and headed across the street. Lily's house was one of those quaint turn-of-the-century structures Pat called a "little-old-lady house." It was a small two-story frame house with a low porch running the length of the front; old-fashioned lace curtains hung in the windless heat of the top-floor windows.

She knocked gently on the front door. Eventually Lily's husband, David, opened the door. It was painfully obvious that he'd just gotten out of bed. Pat stammered hello.

Finally Lily came downstairs. Her short hair was combed but wet and her clothes looked thrown on. She was clearly surprised to see Pat on her porch, more than three hours early for the party.

Pat handed the bottle of wine to Lily. "Happy housewarming!"

Lifting the bottle from the sack and noting the cheap brand, Lily said, "Oh, thanks. We have more in the kitchen. For later."

Was the better wine meant for the other guests or was that a nasty poke at Pat's early drinking? Pat wasn't sure and didn't care. She only knew the fear was still there, so she still wasn't drunk enough. How was she going to get Lily to open the bottle in her hand?

Pat followed Lily up the steep stairs and was treated to a tour of the new apartment. It consisted of a small dark kitchen, a tiny bathroom, a single bedroom, and a living room. The bedroom was filled with an old-fashioned iron bed, a huge wardrobe, and a large desk.

The rooms seemed very small until they went into the sparsely furnished living room, which seemed impossibly large for a house that looked so small and dainty from the outside. There was no explanation for Pat's distorted perception and she saw it as one more piece of evidence that her mental capacities were deteriorating.

Pat limped to the Danish-modern sofa and sat down while Lily went off to find socks and Band-Aids for her feet.

When Lily returned, she found Pat staring into space, tears streaming down her face. Alarmed, she asked, "What's wrong?" She put her fine-boned hands on her old friend's shoulder. At Lily's touch, Pat broke into loud sobs.

Overhearing the outburst, David walked in and knelt down beside them. "Anything I can do?" he asked kindly.

"David, I . . ." Pat started in a small cracking voice. "I don't know what year it is. I'm pretty sure it's not 1963, but it seems like it is."

Pat watched with horror as David's expression of sympathy shifted to one of bafflement and then... What? Shock? Disappointment? Fear? Oh, my God, Pat thought, he thinks I'm crazy.

David quickly recovered his composure. "Are you serious? You don't know what year it is?"

"Can't seem to come up with it," Pat chirped idiotically.

After an awkward silence, Lily said, "Well, I better start dinner." She backed away from the two people, now sitting uncomfortably at opposite ends of the sofa, and turned toward the kitchen. "Can I get you anything?"

"A drink," said Pat wryly.

David poured out two glasses of wine; he and Pat took hefty swallows. Then Pat could stand it no longer. She turned to him and said simply, "I know this is stupid, but what year *is* it?"

David answered, "It's June 4, 1968."

Pat looked at him blankly and shook her head. What he'd said just didn't sound right. Not only the year but the whole date. But it's hot, she thought. It *is* summer. David must be right.

She tried to get it all fixed in her mind, but then her six-fingered hands drew her attention again. Her hands had moved of their own accord and all she could think about was getting those fingers counted....

Finally understanding that she was not going to respond, David got up and walked away. Pat was silent for the next couple of hours, while David helped Lily out and busied himself at the stereo, choosing records. Guests could start arriving at any time now. Seeing that Pat had moved from the sofa to the floor and was completely absorbed in her own strange thoughts, David decided to leave her alone.

Eventually people came, food was served and eaten, more wine was drunk. Music and polite conversation flowed. But all of it was a blur to Pat, who remained sprawled on the floor for hours, drinking, smoking, and studying her fingers.

As the hour grew late, one by one the guests drifted out the door. Oddly, Pat finally became alert and animated. Though she'd been drinking steadily throughout the evening—and undoubtedly they all thought she was completely soused—she did not feel drunk. But the agonizing fears and the pounding heart had at last subsided. Which, after all, was what she'd been trying to accomplish since she woke up.

When Pat realized that the last guest was leaving, she stood up and teetered precariously on one leg and then the other as she pulled on her boots.

"Why don't you let David take you home? I don't like the idea of you walking by yourself," Lily said. As if on cue, David appeared in the doorway, wearing motorcycle boots and a helmet.

It was one o'clock in the morning by the time they arrived at the huge, oddly pieced-together Victorian home that Pat and John lived in. Only the porch light was on. Pat got off the motorcycle but made no move.

"Can we talk for a little while?" she asked in what she knew was a pleading voice.

David heaved a deep sigh. "I have to be getting back. Lily will be worried. Uh, Pat, I really think you should talk to John."

He left her standing on the porch. Wearily Pat climbed the wide wooden stairs to the second floor and stepped into the darkness. Their two-room apartment consisted of a kitchen and a tiny bedroom. The bedroom door was closed, signifying that John was home but sound asleep.

Pat steeled herself to be as quiet as possible. In spite of the fact that not ten minutes earlier she had been desperate for someone to talk to, that was the last thing she wanted now. She turned the knob silently and crept into the shadowy room.

She eased herself into the bed; the springs groaned loudly under her weight. John, a light sleeper, mumbled. Pat ignored him, snuggling deeper into the bed, hoping to find a safe warm spot. But without success. John woke up.

"You okay? How was the party?" He started to turn on a light.

"Don't, please. I'm too tired." Pat pulled the sheet over her head. "We'll talk tomorrow."

John agreed. But just as he was lapsing into a comfortable doze, he was startled awake. He realized Pat was crying. He reached out and put his arms around her.

"Something's wrong!" she blurted suddenly, rising on one arm and staring wildly out the open window. She wailed, in a voice filled with fear and sorrow, "Oh, my God, what is it?"

"What is it, Pat? What's the matter?" he pleaded, holding her tighter with every agonized cry she made.

In a moment or two she was able to catch her breath; she gasped, "I don't know, but something terrible is happening. Something horrible!"

"Can you tell me about it?" he asked frantically, trying to make himself heard over her cries.

John's voice sounded distant and Pat could barely make out his words. She was too busy trying to make sense of the agonizing emotions and images crashing around in her head. She wanted to leap out of the bed and run screaming into the street. Then suddenly she fell completely silent.

John felt her body stiffen and he drew back automatically, as though he'd unexpectedly come upon not a sleeping body but a dead one. Pat was staring out the window toward the southern horizon—barely visible as

14

a jagged line of treetops at the edge of the Kaw Valley—
but he knew she was not admiring the view. Her eyes
were focused on some scene far more distant.

"Tell me what you see," he said in a hoarse whis-
per, but he wasn't at all sure he really wanted to know.

"Something awful, something really awful, is
happening—and I don't know what it is. I don't know
where it's coming from!" Her voice became more hysterical with every word, but she just couldn't help it.

"Maybe you can get a fix on where it's coming
from. I mean, literally, from what direction," John
suggested in what he hoped was a rational voice.

Even before the last words were uttered, a peculiar sensation manifested itself along the side of Pat's
body. A "tingling pressure" was the only way she could
describe it to herself. She saw it falling against her like
the beam from a spotlight, which hit only the parts of
her body facing it and left the rest of her in shadow.

In a much calmer voice she said, "I think it's
coming from west of here, and a little bit south."

John watched as she continued to stare out the
window into the darkness. "Is it here in town, or
farther away?"

"No, not here." What she couldn't say—because
everything was happening too fast—was that she'd
begun a journey and had flown over the ragged ranges
and forests of the Rocky Mountains of Colorado and was
quickly making her mental/visual way across the Ne-
vada deserts.

A new wave of panic overtook her as the yellowish
glow on the far western horizon signaled the approach
to "Nightmare City," the name she and an artist friend
named Franny Lehrman had given to Los Angeles
several years before. Franny had a crush on some
obscure actor whose name Pat couldn't remember . . .

In real time, only a few seconds had passed. It was
now 2 A.M. As soon as Pat realized that the sickly

glow—rapidly becoming a garish glare—zooming toward her *was* Los Angeles, she told John.

"What do you see? What's happening."

"Oh, no . . . it's him," she suddenly burst out. "It's Franny's actor!"

"Franny who?" John asked, bewildered. He was always amazed at how little they knew of each other's pasts.

Pat fell silent, staring through wide wet eyes into the blackness. She watched mesmerized as the actor's face gave way to Franny's face, and she understood that the actor was not the source of her compulsion, and neither was Franny. This thing had nothing whatsoever to do with them.

John shivered with the chill that came over him at the sound of Pat's voice—now low, hoarse, deadly serious. Compared to the hysterical tenor of her voice just moments before, this voice was from an entirely different person.

"His eyes . . ." she said. "He has these dark, shiny eyes. He's looking right at me . . . his eyes are small and round . . . and, oh, he's crying. He's scared to death . . . and he's so terribly, terribly sad. Dark curly hair, short and curly. Dark eyebrows, darkish skin, swarthy-looking, like from the Middle East, an Arab or something. He's small, short and thin. Almost like a little boy, except for the eyes. Full of anger and terror and sadness. The most terrible sadness I've ever seen."

The silence crashed deafeningly around the tiny bedroom. John felt her body shaking gently in renewed but now much softer sobbing. Fresh hot streams of tears glistened down her cheeks. She glanced sideways at him for an instant, and he realized that she was back. Then she closed her eyes and sank down into the bed and fell into the even breathing of sleep.

Just before she sank into unconsciousness, she thought she heard him say, "Pat, who was it? Do you know who it was?"

The next morning a terrible thirst and the first throbbings of a king-size headache hit Pat as she stirred from a dead sleep. She heard the rustling of newspapers and a weak "ahem" from the foot of the bed, so she turned over and stuffed her face into the pillow.

John cleared his throat louder this time. "Are you awake?"

"No!"

"Well, I think you ought to see this," he said with some urgency. "I've been waiting and waiting for you to wake up, and you ought to see this *now*."

He walked around to the side of the bed where Pat lay. He folded the newspaper over, so that a large photograph could easily be seen. "I guess you already know all about this."

Pat squinted up from the pillow. There was a frighteningly serious look on John's face. "What do you mean?" she asked, suddenly not sure she wanted to know. Without waiting for an answer, she looked at the picture.

"Oh, my God." Glaring wild-eyed and mad from the blurry newsprint photo was the face of the man she'd seen last night.

"It's him, isn't it?" It was more of a statement than a question. "His name is Sirhan Sirhan. He shot Bobby Kennedy last night—actually, early this morning . . . in Los Angeles. There's a two-hour time difference between here and California. It happened while you were telling me about it."

"Is Kennedy dead?" she asked, staring at the photo.

"He's in bad shape, but still alive. It doesn't look good, though."

"What's today's date?" she asked, gulping for air. She began to cry again.

"It's June 5," John replied.

17

"He won't live past tomorrow," she said with finality, recalling the finger-counting—one, two, three, four, five, six . . .

"Do you want me to leave you alone so you can go back to sleep?" he asked gently.

"Yes, please," she answered. "And, John . . . I don't want you to tell me anything more about this. No hospital reports, no police reports, nothing . . . okay?"

John agreed and left. Pat turned toward the wall, pulled the sheet over her head, and prayed for sleep.

On June 6, 1968, at 1:15 A.M., Robert F. Kennedy was pronounced dead of a gunshot wound inflicted by a lone assassin in the city of Los Angeles.

For twenty years Pat did not talk about what had happened. She eventually divorced John and lost touch with Lily. By 1988 she was living with her second husband in Staten Island, New York, and was involved in the publishing industry. Lee Chapman, a magazine editor, introduced her to literary agent Sharon Jarvis. They discussed their mutual interest in publishing and somehow the topic of supernatural stories came up. Hesitantly Pat talked about the odd experiences of a "friend" and eventually confessed she'd had the experiences herself.

It wasn't until November 1988 that Pat and Lee actually sat down to write Pat's story. It was an emotionally wrenching task and took several weeks to put down on paper; they brought the manuscript to Sharon later that month. Since there was no rush to read it, Sharon put it to one side of her desk. But the next day, looking at the manuscript, she felt a compulsion to read and edit it. In fact, she feverishly worked over the manuscript all afternoon and evening. While she worked, as was her habit, the radio was on in the background.

Suddenly, in the midst of reading, Sharon stopped, startled. All the radio stations were running special programs dedicated to the memory of John F. Kennedy—and as Sharon read, his death was ghoulishly replayed over and over again, not only on paper but also live, on radio.

This was November 22, 1988, the twenty-fifth anniversary of his assassination. . . .

Dark Shadows

Statistics tell us that the most popular creature of all time, in books and movies, is the vampire. As a result, people have many preconceived notions about what a vampire is and does.

Stephen Kaplan, founder of the Vampire Research Center, has attempted to define the modern vampire, through years of research and interviews with those who claim to be vampires. An acknowledged expert in the paranormal—he was the first to reveal the truth behind the Amityville Horror—he lectures and appears on radio and television all over the United States and Canada.

As a result, he attended a most bizarre convention where the subject of vampires was paramount, and so three unlikely people found themselves sharing the same stage: the vampire hunter, the actor who played a vampire, and the real thing. . . .

Dark Shadows, television's first "horror" soap opera, first aired in June 1966, over the ABC-TV network. The show went on to become one of daytime TV's most popular series, and during its high point had an audience of almost twenty million fans. It also spawned a series of books and several feature films.

When the show began, it was somewhat like a gothic romance. Its early stories featured the ghosts of women who had killed themselves by jumping off a cliff—

Widow's Hill—into the sea. The voices of these spirits would lure new—and usually lovesick—victims to that same cliff and urge them to jump too.

There was also a bizarre character, a woman who was a "phoenix." She would die a flaming death every hundred years, only to return and lure innocent victims into the flames with her. As you can see, the show was pretty unusual, and getting more so. . . .

In 1967 and 1968, respectively, the characters of Barnabas Collins and Quentin Collins were introduced, and the show took a profitable turn for the worse. For Barnabas (played by the noted Shakespearean actor Jonathan Frid) was a vampire, and Quentin a werewolf. In fact, the plots began to weave through several generations of the Collins family, many of whose members were less than—or more than—human. Vampires, witches, mad scientists, Gypsies, ghosts, and the world of the supernatural became the dominant elements.

Barnabas Collins was not your usual vampire, however. He was fairly unhappy about his circumstances, though when he was first released from his chained coffin he was quite frightening. Barnabas had been turned into a vampire by a former lover who just happened to be a jealous witch. He spent the next four years of the show searching for a way to lift the curse, while his character was transformed from a monster to a guilt-ridden good guy who felt badly each time he needed to drink blood. Barnabas, the sexy, sympathetic vampire, became the darling of the fans, and women went wild.

Since the story line covered many generations, from the eighteenth through the twentieth century, there were numerous costume changes—which were later reflected in the clothing worn by fans attending *Dark Shadows* conventions.

The *Dark Shadows* conventions first began in the 1970s on the West Coast; the first East Coast convention was held in 1983 by dedicated fans who were thrilled to see their favorite show brought back, even if it was in reruns. Fan clubs had names like the Alternate Shadows, the Collinsport Call, Inside the Old House, Shades of Grayson, ShadowGram, and the World of Dark Shadows. In fact, all these fan clubs joined forces in 1984 to put on the second annual convention during Veterans Day weekend at the Gateway Hilton in Newark, New Jersey. The guest of honor was Jonathan Frid, who had played Barnabas until the show went off the air in April 1971. (Frid has cheerfully attended the conventions every year since.) The guest lecturer was—appropriately—Dr. Stephen Kaplan, founder of the Vampire Research Center. Neither the imaginary vampire nor the vampire hunter realized until much later that a real vampire was also in attendance. . . .

Dr. Stephen Kaplan and his wife, Roxanne Salch Kaplan, pushed through the revolving doors of the Gateway Hilton. It was Saturday, November 10, 1984, and two members of the Alternate Shadows Fan Club had driven the Kaplans door-to-door. Stephen and Roxanne were confronted by an assortment of vampires, werewolves, and ghosts—the usual supernatural characters from the show. But there were also jewel-bedecked Gypsies, rotting corpses, Victorian ladies of the Gay Nineties, flappers, and groups of "mourners" appropriately dressed for a funeral.

Dr. Kaplan wore a black pin-stripe three-piece suit, in contrast to the costumed fans, and carried his briefcase, which contained the lecture he would give that afternoon. He felt that he had to project a very professional image because of the sensational nature of his work. By 1984 Dr. Kaplan had already devoted thirteen years to the study of the supernatural in general and vampires in particular.

Kaplan was carefully prepared to lecture the *Dark Shadows* fans about vampires, planning to disguise his descriptions of the vampirelike people who had contacted his organization in the past. As a social scientist, he had to protect the privacy of those whose families would be threatened by such a disclosure. He also had to choose his information very carefully, not wanting his special research to be stolen and used by people who had not worked for it.

The Kaplans entered the large hotel lobby, checked in, unpacked, and then took an elevator to the floor where the convention was being held. There were special programs going on all day long and hundreds of fans were already milling about. Dr. Kaplan was scheduled to take part in a "Vampire Symposium," which would begin at ten A.M. and last for about three hours.

Down the hall were several rooms where different events were taking place simultaneously. One room contained a projector and screen, where episodes—many of them not seen in decades—were being shown around the clock. One of the reels was a special "blooper" reel, showing the actors flubbing their lines and cutting up.

Another room contained an art show, where fans displayed drawings and paintings of their favorite characters and actors. There seemed to be an inordinate number of pictures of Barnabas Collins, the vampire. Perhaps it was because Jonathan Frid was the guest of honor, but no doubt it was also because his character was so popular.

Yet another room was the "dealers" room, where all sorts of *Dark Shadows* memorabilia was on sale. Books, movie posters, T-shirts, photographs of the actors, and more. The Kaplans had arranged to have a table available there, where they could disseminate information about their organizations, their research, and their literature.

Later on in the convention there would be a costume show, which the guests would judge. In addition to Jonathan Frid, two other actors who had appeared on the show were putting in appearances. A "reunion jubilee" was planned as well. That would be a party where the fans could meet the actors, get their autographs, and have their photographs taken standing next to their favorite character.

Also in the evenings were small gatherings where fans brought musical instruments and serenaded each other with "filksongs." (This was a typographical error that had appeared years ago on a program listing at a science-fiction convention. Of course it was supposed to be "folksongs" and the misnomer had stuck ever since. Usually, instead of folksongs, fans would take existing music and add their own lyrics.) In this case, the songs would be about *Dark Shadows*, all its characters, and the convoluted plot lines.

The convention had actually begun Friday, the day before, when a busload of fans traveled to Tarrytown, New York, to explore a 147-year-old Gothic fortress where the two *Dark Shadows* movies were filmed. Friday evening was a gala celebration for the official opening of the convention, where two committee members, dressed as characters from the show, introduced the guests of the convention. Other than Jonathan Frid, however, the panelists for the Vampire Symposium were not there until Saturday.

Since they had time before the symposium began, the Kaplans and their assistant, Brian, brought their paraphernalia to the table and began organizing their material. Several people who knew the Kaplans came over to the table to chat. Among them was a young man named Thomas whom Stephen had met at an occult bookshop that also sold items of black magic. The young man was very excited and Stephen wondered why.

"I'm hoping," said Thomas, "to meet the vampire and give her some of my blood."

Stephen thought Thomas meant he was in a play or skit that the convention was presenting.

"No, no," said Thomas, grinning. "*She*'s here and she needs human volunteers. I pray that I am chosen!''

On that odd note, Stephen looked at his watch. He was scheduled shortly to preside over the symposium, so he and Roxanne made their way to the large chair-filled room where it would be held. At the front of the room was a long table with several microphones. Joining him at the dais were Jonathan Frid and Jim Knusch, an occult researcher and film historian. Each was to give a separate speech, and afterward there would be an open forum.

Jim Knusch's appearance at the convention was as an eleventh-hour replacement for a member of the Count Dracula Society who was to have lectured on the vampire in literature. Jim's professional credentials were excellent and he'd been recommended to the convention committee by Dr. Kaplan. In fact, Jim had given lectures at Dr. Kaplan's Parapsychology Institute of America.

Jim Knusch spoke about the vampire in cinema, the classic renditions, the variations and modern adaptations, and peppered his talk with interesting tidbits and trivia. The first film appearance of the vampire, he said, was in a 1914 silent movie, *A Fool There Was*, starring Theda Bara (whose name was an anagram for "Arab Death"). The movie had been inspired by Rudyard Kipling's poem *The Vampire*, which was about a woman who drains her hapless male victims not of blood but of free will and common sense. The shortened term for "vampire" was "The Vamp," by which name Theda Bara herself was known for the rest of her career, Knusch pointed out.

At this comment, a young green-eyed brunette in the audience shook her head negatively. Her long dark hair swung to and fro with the movement. She had a long, thin face and hair that fell about her shoulders. The dress she wore was a bit old-fashioned, but then again, a great many of the attendees were in costume.

"Without question," stated Knusch, "the most famous screen partaker of blood is Count Dracula. And the most famous silent screen rendition of the vampire appeared in a German production titled *Nosferatu,* starring horror star Max Schreck, whose last name translates in German as 'fright.'''

Adjusting his wire-rimmed glasses, Knusch then talked about the vampire in the early sound movies of the 1930's. First, from Hollywood, came *Dracula,* starring Bela Lugosi. Knusch pointed out that, interestingly, in this film and all subsequent films that Lugosi appeared in as a vampire, he never wore fangs. The second movie was a Danish film, *Vampyr,* which drew on local beliefs and folklore and showed the vampire as an old woman.

Stephen Kaplan decided to begin his lecture, "Do Vampires Really Exist?", with the vampire "colonies" that had been reported in Texas, Ohio, Florida, California, Massachusetts, New York, and Pennsylvania. He also talked about being contacted by vampires from as far away as Guam and as close as Queens, New York, where he lived.

In the audience, the striking young lady with the long hair smirked knowingly at the mention of her home state— California—which was so enlightened that it had already proclaimed May 28 as California Vampire Day.

Intrigued by the variety and diversity of those claiming to be vampires, Dr. Kaplan had instituted a "Vampire Census" in an effort to categorize, identify, and classify the modern vampire. For instance, he was able, based on the data, to come up with a general description of your average vampire. The Vampire Research Center also had been sent photographs by many people who were responding to his Vampire Census, and so Dr. Kaplan was in sole possession of a small but fascinating collection of photos of modern vampires that had never been seen before, with one exception. He'd shown them on television in Cleveland when he'd done the *Morning Exchange* program.

After the show, they'd been returned to a special locked file.

"A female vampire looks to be in her early twenties but is really at least twice as old," Kaplan told the audience. "She has green eyes, blond hair, and is about five feet, eight inches tall."

At this, the tall brunette woman from California smiled again.

"The average male vampire also looks to be in his early twenties," Kaplan continued, "but is closer to fifty. He is likely to have blue eyes, brown hair, and be five feet, ten inches tall."

Kaplan explained that there were different species of vampires. "Psychic vampires do not drink blood. They are the opposite of faith healers and take the energy from the bodies of others in order to survive."

Psychic vampires used a metaphysical ability that almost anyone could develop. They were closer to ordinary humans and did not live as long as blood-drinking vampires. Vampirelike individuals behaved in many ways like real vampires, but while they relished blood, they had no actual physical need for human blood. Nor were vampires necessarily evil and vicious creatures waiting to attack in the night.

As he spoke, Kaplan wondered if he could spot Thomas' vampire by looks alone, or if she would give herself away by asking a telling question. His eyes searched the audience, but there were many people and some of the seats were far away.

"However," Dr. Kaplan said, "real vampires have a physical need for blood—they must have it! They need to drink several ounces of blood every week. If they don't get it, they won't necessarily die but they will age."

Dr. Kaplan felt that vampires could live for several centuries, because of their genetic composition and their need for blood, to which their metabolism was geared.

The lady in the audience licked her lips.

The vampire of movies, books, and television was not necessarily the vampire that roamed dark streets. Dr. Kaplan said there were many similarities: the outstanding beauty of their alabaster skins and seductive, sensuous looks, which drew victims to them (in fact, exchanging sexual favors *and* blood was common); the personal charm, knowledge, and wealth acquired over hundreds of years; a preference for coffins; intolerance of sunlight; and an overpowering need for blood.

The dissimilarities were: he'd never seen any fangs; he believed that vampires were merely exceptionally long-lived, not immortal; they usually wore ordinary street clothes (rather than black garments and capes) because they did not want to draw attention to themselves; they did not cower from crucifixes.

Nor would they stay away if you hung garlic in your windows. You would have to *eat* the garlic, because that was the only thing guaranteed to turn a scent-sensitive vampire's stomach! Eating garlic changes the blood chemistry, so that, not only would a person smell different to a vampire, but a vampire would know the blood it might drink would therefore taste different and not be digestible.

Nor had he ever seen a vampire transform into a bat; in fact, should a so-called Dracula make such a claim, "then I know he's auditioning for the *Gong Show*."

With fang firmly in cheek, Dr. Kaplan needed a sense of humor to separate the kooks, charlatans, and crazies from the real vampires. (One of his favorite stories involved a man attacked by a midget vampire on stilts.) But he was seriously worried that many of these unstable Dracula fetishists would try to rip out his throat. And he'd also received death threats from blood cults, who were involved in more horrendous crimes than merely taking a few ounces of blood from a sometimes willing victim. He no longer held interviews in his home. He would conduct his research only in public places, "like McDonald's, Roy Rogers', or this convention."

Then Jonathan Frid discussed his role as the vampire Barnabas Collins in *Dark Shadows*. "I'm sorry that we're not talking about real vampires," he commented almost sadly. Frid, a distinguished gentleman in his fifties, emphasized the fact that he was *not* Barnabas, but rather an actor playing a part.

Portraying a vampire for television was quite different and sometimes uncomfortable. For instance, when wearing stage fangs, he could not talk clearly and his lines sounded like mush. In order to be understood, he had to do the vampire version of a quick-change act. He would speak his lines off-camera, and then, while the camera would show the victim's reaction, he'd whip out the fake fangs, slip them in his mouth, and then, with the camera back on him, bite his victim.

Kaplan, who was the technical adviser for the off-Broadway play *The Passion of Dracula*, knew about the problems of acting while wearing fangs. For that play, however, they'd obtained a smaller set made by a dentist, so that the actor had less difficulty in talking.

Jim Knusch explained that in movies, dubbing was often done. This was long after the scenes had been filmed, and the actor, in a recording studio, would voice-over his lines, making them clearer. Or sometimes, during filming an assistant would stand on the sidelines holding the fangs. At the appropriate moment in the movie, the camera would be stopped and the assistant would run over and put the fangs in the actor's mouth.

Jonathan Frid also had a problem lying down in a coffin. For some reason, the prop men had bought a coffin for the show that was too short, and Jonathan wouldn't fit into it unless he scrunched down. Then, while shoehorned into the coffin, the lid would close and smack him in the knees!

Another time, Frid was to play a scene in which he was to rise out of the coffin. He climbed into it and awaited instructions from the director, but first the crew had to do some light and camera-angle adjustments. The crew took a very long time . . . and Frid fell asleep. The director had to wake him up to play the scene, and that was the closest Frid had ever come to true coffin slumber.

These stories led into a very bizarre discussion of coffins and their cost. Kaplan thought that most vampires probably spent thousands of dollars on fancy coffins, since it would be terrible to spend the next hundred years or so in lousy quarters or be homeless. Vampires probably bought coffins that were guaranteed leakproof as well. Jim Knusch launched into a long examination of the kinds of coffins used in films—from Bela Lugosi through Frank Langella—and a comparison of American and European coffins.

About 12:15 P.M., Patrick Garrison, one of the founders of the Alternate Shadows Fan Club, introduced the Open Forum, during which the three panel members would field all kinds of questions from the audience. Patrick was wearing the traditional vampire garb of a black cape lined in crimson. Most of the attention was focused on Jonathan Frid by his adoring fans, and the majority of the questions during the discussion were directed toward him. By this time, the unusual young lady from California had risen and left, with several young men trailing in her wake.

The Open Forum lasted for an hour, after which Kaplan sought out Patrick and his wife, Josette, and asked about the female vampire who supposedly was at the convention, looking for human volunteers.

"She's here," confirmed Patrick. "You know her."

Kaplan was surprised.

"Yes," said Patrick. "It's Misty, from California."

Strangely enough, the Kaplans had been on the West Coast just weeks earlier for an appearance on San Francisco's *People Are Talking*. Then they had flown to San Diego to interview Misty, a "real" vampire, with whom they'd been corresponding since 1982. This same vampire was now present at the convention.

Kaplan had heard rumors that Misty might attend, but she'd told him she didn't have the air fare, and she was worried for her safety. Apparently New York and Newark had fearful reputations and made her nervous. There was also the problem of her need for human blood. The convention committee decided that if Misty could dine on willing volunteers, she need not walk the streets of New York or Newark in the dead of night. The convention had paid her air fare and the Garrisons were letting her stay at their house. But during the convention she was using their hotel suite, getting her nourishment. As word spread through the convention, the line outside her suite grew. It reminded Kaplan of suitors lining up to fill in a young lady's dance card.

Not everyone at the convention was happy about Misty's appearance. One worried mother of a young man who was on the waiting line upstairs asked Dr. Kaplan to meet her in one of the rooms.

"What happens to a person bitten by a 'real' vampire?" she asked. She admitted that her son was a volunteer and that she was worried about the aftereffects. She wanted to know if vampires were diseased crazy people on drugs. She was also afraid that if her son was bitten too many times, he would become a vampire too.

Kaplan knew that if her son was over twenty-one years of age he could not be stopped from giving himself to a vampire. But he promised the distraught woman he would investigate what was happening.

Stephen and Roxanne took the elevator to the Garrisons' suite. Misty was there, and the line was still outside.

Because she would be indoors during the convention, Misty did not have to wear protective clothing. If she did go outside during the day, she had to wear sunglasses and long sleeves or lotions that blocked out the sun's ultraviolet rays.

Misty had been in the hotel suite since November 9. She was shy about being among so many people and had relied on the Garrisons to guide her through the convention, though she was in a festive mood, because the *Dark Shadows* convention coincided with her birthday—November 10th. She was not used to large crowds and had always been a loner, even as a child. She spent most of her time indoors and had few friends.

Misty remembered watching *Dark Shadows* with her grandmother, particularly a scene in one show where Barnabas, the vampire, and Quentin, the werewolf, met face-to-face in the night, fangs bared. Later in the show, Barnabas attacked a young woman. Misty's grandmother was disturbed by these scenes and turned off the television. But Misty wasn't sure if it was because of the way vampires were being depicted or because she was afraid Misty would go out and attack someone.

Misty (who incidentally sported a tattoo of a firebat on her left arm) had a nice set of teeth and small, sharp fangs. She told the Kaplans that people had come up to her throughout the convention, begging to be bitten. One woman bowed to her and called her "Countess." She had no worries about not feeding, and felt that people cared for her by offering themselves. In fact, she had more people than she needed. Although it was a full moon, when she was usually hungrier, Misty had already gotten enough blood from three or four volunteers. Just a few ounces from each. But she didn't have the heart to tell the rest of the volunteers, waiting in line, that she couldn't take another bite.

Nor had she had sex with any of the donors. She preferred exchanges of gifts, money, and friendship. On

Dark Shadows

that particular day, all Misty had given was back rubs; it was her way of relaxing a donor. If the person flinched at all when she bit him, she would stop immediately.

One of the donors, a young woman, had asked Misty to kill her. She wanted to die in the arms of a vampire. Misty refused. It was not her style to attack people and drain them of blood. It wasn't necessary. The most she'd ever taken from a person was about one pint of blood every two weeks. However, she often needed to feed daily.

She preferred to bite willing donors; it made her feel closer to them. And it meant getting the blood fresh, from the bite, not later, when it had congealed. Misty also had a few favorite spots for biting: the neck, of course, and the inner bend of an arm. Rarely did she use a razor or a syringe. She would not bite anyone who was sick; she was able to tell by smell. Her immunity system would be affected by the immunity of the person she fed from.

Instead of rejecting the rest of the people waiting, she was giving them a little love bite. Perhaps it was the vampire equivalent of an autograph. Kaplan now felt that the worried mother of the boy in line had nothing to worry about.

Misty agreed to send the volunteers to Kaplan's table in the dealers' room, after their experience with her, so that Kaplan could interview them. Both Kaplans left Misty's suite, followed by some of the volunteers. Each one, male and female, felt that the bite was a mark of distinction. Most of the volunteers were attractive young men and women who told Stephen they felt no pain. In fact, they all liked Misty, and some would become her pen pals, subscribing to her journal. Others would meet after the convention for further experimentation. Misty had formed a small select group called Lost Shadows, which had twenty-five members, mostly male, most of them vampires. Members were all over the United States and Canada.

That evening, Misty and the Kaplans went to dinner together. She told them that she still had her specially built coffin in the living room of her home in California. It was a bit worn by then, but very soft, of crushed velvet. She was publishing a newsletter, *The Vampire's Journal*, and also working on her autobiography. She wanted people to know that vampires were not like the vampires depicted in popular entertainment. She did not like vampire movies and thought they gave people the wrong idea. In Lost Shadows, the group she led, violence was not allowed, and any member who caused the death of a donor would be banned.

Afterward, the Kaplans decided they'd had enough excitement and retired for a quiet night.

The next morning, they were having breakfast in the hotel restaurant when two young ladies in their twenties approached Stephen for his autograph. Both had marks on their necks.

"I wonder," Stephen said to Roxanne, "just how many people she's bitten?"

In the dealers' room, their old acquaintance Thomas showed up again. He was despondent because he had not been selected as a volunteer. Apparently a vampire hickey was no substitute for the real thing. He left in search of Misty.

If he'd stayed, he might have gotten what he wanted. Misty did come to the dealers' room and walked around relatively unnoticed.

At one of the tables near the Kaplans', two young men, Joe Sena and Tom Powers, were trying to sell an assortment of vampire memorabilia, some of it directly related to *Dark Shadows*, including a small packet of calling cards for the show's characters: "Barnabas Collins, Vampire. Available for Blood Drives. Night Hours Only."

They were also selling a comic book they had created and published, called *Doc Dorian*, about a mysterious fellow who hunted down and killed vampires. Joe and Tom had mistakenly assumed that a convention based on a television show about vampires would be an ideal place to sell their comic. Unfortunately they miscalculated and found business to be slow—except for the sale of those calling cards. Desperate for customers, even strange fans, they tried to talk to everyone who passed the table.

A striking brunette with very pale skin, dressed all in black, approached the table. Tom shot Joe a "here-comes-another-weirdo" look.

The woman asked about the comic book. Joe replied that it was an action-adventure story about a vampire hunter.

Her head snapped up and she stared at Joe. "Oh," she breathed, "I would never want to read anything about someone who *killed* vampires. Do you believe in vampires?" she added softly.

Joe stammered and mumbled.

"Well, *I'm* a vampire," she said, and dramatically stalked off.

Sometime after this incident, Stephen and Roxanne attended Jonathan Frid's dramatic readings. They observed Misty sitting in the audience. She was surrounded on every side by an entourage, all of whom had bites on their necks. By Misty's estimate, she'd bitten nearly two hundred people.

When the convention was over, everyone went home, but Misty's influence lingered on. Dr. Kaplan received a phone call from a beautiful young lady from Pittsburgh who had attended the convention. Ever since she had been bitten by Misty, she had been drinking human blood from other volunteers who also had been at the convention. She now lusted for it and claimed that she was most affected during the full moon. She said she had developed small fangs, which were getting longer. At the same time, she felt healthier than ever. Her boyfriends had accepted this new way of life and were also contributing blood when she needed it.

Other convention attendees had been similarly affected. Was this the beginning of a possible epidemic? Suddenly Kaplan remembered that the convention had been held during a full moon. . . .

In April of the following year, also during a full moon, the phone rang in the Kaplan house. Stephen, just home from work, answered it.

"Hello," said an ominous male voice. "Is this the Vampire Research Center?"

"Yes," said Kaplan. "How can I help you?"

"Well, I'm a vampire and I live in California—"

"San Diego, right?" said Stephen. "I know. You're not the first and I'm sure you won't be the last."

"Steve?" Roxanne interrupted. "I forgot to tell you. We also got calls this week from Toronto, Boston, Cleveland, and San Francisco."

Kaplan hung up the phone and turned to Roxanne. "It's time we hid out in Bermuda again."

Roxanne nodded. She could use a vacation, as long as they consulted a calendar and didn't go anywhere during a full moon. . . .

A Ghost Forevermore

This bizarre account comes from the files of the Parapsychology Institute of America, founded by Stephen Kaplan. He and his wife, Roxanne, have traveled throughout the North American continent in search of the supernatural. But the strangest part of this story took place not far from their own home.

None of the participants' names have been changed and all the details are true, including the picture of the traveling ghost. I have seen the odd photograph myself, the photo that shows a spectral form rocking for eternity. . . .

Edgar Allan Poe was born in Boston, Massachusetts, on January 19, 1809. Two years later he was orphaned in Richmond, Virginia, by the death of his widowed mother, an English actress. A year later, the rich but childless Mrs. Allan adopted Edgar, against the wishes of her husband, John Allan, a wealthy merchant.

Mrs. Allan took Edgar to England and placed him in a school near London, where he stayed until 1826, when he went back to the United States to attend the University of Virginia. Edgar and his adoptive father were never close, and frequent arguments with John Allan caused Poe to run away after one year of school. While in England, Poe had begun to write, and in 1827—the same year he joined the army—his first poem, *Tamerlane*, was published in Boston. (In 1829, the poem *Al Aaraaf* was published in

Baltimore.) Poe remained "employed" by the United States government until 1831, probably the longest time he remained with a single employer.

The last three months of this period were spent as a cadet at the Military Academy at West Point. Poe was summarily dismissed from the Academy for behavior unbecoming to an officer and a gentleman. There is a story passed on by cadets to this day that Poe had been dressed down because he neglected to have certain insignia on his uniform. The next day he appeared for inspection with the insignia, but without the uniform, or any other garments. His dismissal occurred shortly afterward.

Despite his personal and family problems, he was able to continue his writing career. In 1831, the year he left West Point, *Poems* was published in New York. Poe collected prizes for a poem and a story in 1833, and in 1835 he became an editor at *The Southern Literary Messenger* in Richmond.

But Poe's growing alcoholism would keep him from steady employment. Poe, an idealist, was perhaps too sensitive to deal with the demands of one position for too long, and eventually poverty plagued him. However, in 1835 he was able to begin a career as a critic, which provided him with an income through many a lean year. But Poe, who was never truly accepted by his family and who had only a few friends, was not able to break his addictions to stimulants and depressants.

Poe's dreams, the foundation for much of his work, took him alternately from fairylands to ghostlands. He was obsessed by the afterlife and by the nature of death. However, for at least a decade he was able to find some peace. In 1836 he married his young cousin, Virginia Clemm. The marriage seemingly relieved his dependence on drugs for many years.

However, when his beloved wife, Virginia, became very ill in 1841, he was drawn back to his addictions. In

1845 Poe's famous poem *The Raven* appeared. Shortly afterward he became the sole editor of the *Broadway Journal* in Philadelphia. But while the magazine prospered, Poe suffered.

In the spring of 1847, Virginia Clemm Poe died, and Poe's depressions grew worse. In his own words, he "became insane, with periods of horrible sanity." Finally, two years later and at the age of forty, after drinking excessive amounts of alcohol, Edgar Allan Poe died in Baltimore from dehydration on October 7, 1849.

Well, at least his body might have died. But did his spirit? His literary spirit lives on in his works, but what about his ghost?

One hundred and thirty years later, the answer would be found by three members of the Parapsychology Institute of America. They hadn't even known that they were embarking on a search for Poe's spirit, but the spirit found them. . . .

Early on the morning of November 10, 1979, two men and a woman were on a train en route from New York City to Baltimore. They were on their way to demonstrate to a Baltimore radio audience that a psychic could discern historical information about places he had never been before.

One of the three was psychic John Krysko, a handsome young man of medium build and dark hair. Krysko was a metaphysical instructor with the Parapsychology Institute of America (PIA). In later years, he would put his talents to use as an investment advisor, working at integrating intuition into business and environmental endeavors.

Across the aisle sat a pretty young brunette, Roxanne Salch Kaplan. Roxanne was the photographer, the secretary, and the co-director of the Institute. She was to record the unusual events that were yet to happen.

Next to her sat a tall blond-haired man, her husband, Stephen Kaplan, noted psychic investigator, parapsychologist, public-relations expert, and coordinator for all the Institute's activities. In essence, he was along for the ride. Professing limited psychic ability, Kaplan was there to monitor and assist Krysko.

When they arrived at the Baltimore railroad station, the three were met by Allan Christian, a talk-show host on local radio station WBAL, and the technicians who would be recording the show. The host would be acting as guide for the threesome through the various sites selected for investigation. The radio-show producers and Christian had chosen a number of well-known Baltimore sites, but all of these locations were kept secret from Krysko and the Kaplans. The idea was to take Krysko to these places and record—on the spot—his live, unrehearsed reactions. Then his findings would be confirmed or denied by the available experts.

The first stop was Hampton House, a national landmark which had been home to the Ridgley family for more than a century. (The family built the plantation house in the late 1700's and occupied it until 1948.) John Krysko took the lead as the group entered the spacious foyer of the historic home. Trailing Krysko were his colleagues, the radio crew, and last, but certainly not least, the National Parks tour guide.

Suddenly, as if his attention had been drawn away, Krysko stopped under a portrait of two children presumed to be from the Hampton family.

"A lady in a picture had two or three children," intoned Krysko. "One of them went to Europe. Her mother weighed heavily on her conscience—she was a burden when she got older. Father passed on first. Image of an athletic, proud man. Gambling aspect. Bit of a maverick. Business problem around 1820's or 1830's—financial crisis—bad crops.

"Captain during the Revolutionary time. James? Joseph? Also something with a W, like maybe Wilma."

Already the group was drawn into the story John Krysko was telling, a story that was not in the tour brochures. But was it true? Krysko was not concerned about what this group considered truth. He was on a psychic trail and was determined to follow it.

As he entered another room, John looked at another portrait of two children. "I sense that there may have been three children," he continued. "The mother was a good storyteller, also wanted to do a lot of things herself, even though she had servants. The lady liked to entertain and do the cooking.

"The man had at least one other brother, an older brother, more conservative, better business sense. This brother had traded with Boston and with Europe. His time comes in most strongly. One of the kids was a little bit violent, had a duel or something like that."

Krysko, now moving as if he were being pulled, led the group up to the attic, where there was a small room called the Ghost Room. He announced he was having palpitations and that he sensed a dark male presence. He also "received" the letter R. Suddenly the tour guide spoke up. The R stood for Eliza Ridgley, a young girl who allegedly died in the Ghost Room.

Missing children, bad times, ghosts and ominous presences—the tragic course of a family's history spread out over several generations and hundreds of years and sensed in just an hour . . . well, John Krysko had to have time to recover.

So it was with relief that the PIA group found that their next stop was the famous Owl Bar at the Belvedere Hotel. The Owl Bar got its name from the two decorative, mechanical owls which flanked the ends of the bar; they had blinking eyes and were used for both a sobriety test and to signal when whiskey was available during Prohibition.

The owls disappeared without a trace when the hotel was closed in 1971, and the new owners spent years searching for them all over the United States. When the bar reopened in 1977, the owls suddenly reappeared, as if put there by a ghostly hand, which had managed to get through several locked doors. Taped to the bar door was a note: "Where we've been, what we've seen, no matter the din, no one will glean. But if your eyes are clear, today you can tell, the owls of Belvedere have returned from Hell."

However, a psychic cannot just "turn it off," and Krysko could feel ghosts such as John Jacob Astor. Shipping and commerce had been discussed there, as well as politics. The radio host confirmed that many political deals were and still are made in the elegant bar.

Feeling restored, the group decided to take the next steps on the ghostly trail.

The next location was Fort McHenry, which dates back to the American Revolution. So far Krysko had only experienced the lives of a family and then the wheelings and dealings of the rich and famous in pleasant surroundings. Now he was faced with decades of emotions and events involving the lives of hundreds of soldiers and their families who had been stationed at the fort while it was in active service.

The group received a very quick tour of the star-shaped fort, which was built in 1776 and used during the War of 1812 and the Civil War. It was the place where the "flag still stood" in Francis Scott Key's national anthem.

The experience was very rough on Krysko, primarily because of the fort's shape. The star has been used by occultists in various ways over the centuries because it is a known focus for many powers. At Fort McHenry, Krysko became all too aware of those powers.

To feel another's death is always terrible, and here Krysko could feel death all around him, magnified. In one particular room he sensed the presence of a soldier slowly dying or being shot. The officer who acted as a tour guide at the fort explained that a lieutenant and a noncommissioned officer were shot in the room. One man had died instantly. Krysko also felt that a woman with some connection to a soldier, probably a wife, had died in the room. Again the guide confirmed that there were several reports in the records of the wife of a wounded soldier being killed there during the War of 1812.

The group was led into the old cells. Krysko stopped. He explained he was seeing someone scratching or marking on the walls. Could it be a prisoner marking time? Krysko felt the soldier was from the Civil War period. He had died a lonely death. (The Kaplans had also been tape-recording John Krysko's comments; when they played back this section afterward, they could hear hollow sounds and a low growling in the background.)

"I didn't want to come in here. I don't like being here," Krysko said of the cells. "I don't mind the other places. But in here there's a really desperate feeling. . . . It's the kind of thing where I almost feel that I want to kill myself."

The group had passed through other cells of the fort, and certainly there had been death surrounding them, violent death taking place during one of the bloodiest periods in our nation's history. However, this room held more.

Krysko said, "This is the only place that I really feel negative about. Even though the other cells had people who died, they weren't like this. This is the kind of place where the soul passes on but just doesn't leave the area."

Soon there was confirmation that John was right. After questioning, the guide related this story:

A private by the name of John Drew, twenty-eight years old, was found asleep on guard duty on the outer battery. He was brought into a cell, where he would stay until he was court-martialed. As he was cleaning the straw out of the cell, before being locked in, Drew smuggled in a musket. After the guards left, he took off his shoe and his sock, stuck his toe in the trigger, and the muzzle in his mouth, and blew his brains out.

Suddenly Krysko lost his detachment. "I want to get out of here right now!"

The guide, reading through the records, related further events. "There were five documented deaths in that cell: two suicides, two hangings, and one by firing squad."

What of the spirits? Do they really roam the fort as Krysko said they might? The guide explained that ghostly manifestations *had* been seen, not only by the fort's military personnel but by their family members and friends, as well.

It was time to move on. The next stop was 203 N. Amity Street, a former home of Edgar Allan Poe. From 1833 to 1835 he had shared the place with his grandmother Poe, his Aunt Maria Clemm, and his cousin (and later, his wife) Virginia.

It was in this place that the tales "Morella," "Bernice," "King Pest," "Shadow," "Mystification," and "Hans Pfall" were written. However, the group was not aware of these facts at the time. There was one unusual fact they did know, however: the day Poe died—October 7—was Roxanne Kaplan's birthday.

Steve Kaplan shadowed Krysko as they walked through the house, up the winding staircase, and into every room. The color of the walls was pale white, and the steps were a faded brown. As they approached the garret room in the attic, both men sensed a loneliness.

Kaplan became aware of feelings that were not typical for him; he was not generally a lonely man. But he had a lonely, caged-up feeling in the tiny and close room. The walls slanted so that a tall person would have to stoop as he walked through. Questions and feelings flooded both men's minds.

Krysko felt there was a hidden manuscript. Kaplan had high hopes of them finding an unpublished work of Poe's—what a radio show that would be! But the feelings were getting too strong to bear, and they had to leave the room.

As they descended the stairs and entered the kitchen on the first floor, the oppressive feelings left them. It was a pleasant, roomy, and airy place and both men could feel a wonderful warmth, as if Poe had been very happy in that room.

Since it was common knowledge that Poe's life had been a sad and often painful one, the group was surprised when Krysko began discussing Poe's happiness.

"I know Edgar Allen Poe, Capricorn that he was, was a pretty dour type, but I get a fairly happy sense. I don't at all get the negative feeling.

"There were friends over. I see them discussing things late at night. The man that is a friend is lighter-haired, more cherubic, a bit happier. Almost like a student. The man goes to Europe or somewhere. Poe is attracted to a young woman. Her father was a banker or something like that."

Kaplan asked if the woman could have been Lenore, namesake of the famous poem, but Krysko replied that he didn't really know who Lenore was.

"Poe is talking to his friend; they were hearty talks. I think he got some early works published here. I see a man helping him get some of those early works published. They were like newspaper articles or short stories. I get an early sense of life. But there are strange feelings of sexuality, repressed sexuality."

And then Krysko suddenly announced, "The spirit of Edgar Allan Poe tells me that he wanders the house looking for a yet unfound manuscript."

A security man who had accompanied the group told them that the house was locked securely at night. Yet on many nights, a flickering light, resembling a candle, would be seen from outside the house by the security guards. The light appeared to travel from room to room. But no one could enter or leave the house until morning, when the guards unlocked the gate. To this day, the mystery of the light has yet to be explained.

Krysko and the Kaplans had spent a great deal of time at the Poe house, and wanted to spend more—a missing manuscript, a clue to the identity of Lenore—but the radio host was insistent that they push on. But Poe was not finished with them yet.

The group was led to the historic Westminster church, located about six blocks from the Poe house, where immediately Krysko felt himself being drawn downstairs. "May we go there right away?" he asked as he headed unerringly for a door, which did indeed lead to the basement, and to a level below that.

They found themselves in the catacombs underneath the church. It was a dark and stagnant place with hundreds of bits of human bones and skulls. Their guide explained that the human bones had been uncovered by recent excavations of the lower levels of the catacombs. While this was enough to stop many a tourist in his tracks, Krysko continued his walk. He sensed that Edgar Allan Poe was calling him, and the pull was strong.

The Kaplans and the radio crew followed Krysko as he exited the catacombs through a door that led outside, to a cemetery. Krysko led them through the graveyard as if guided by an invisible force.

Suddenly, he turned and pointed to a large tombstone. The group stood still, staring in wonder. It was the marker of the original burial site of Edgar Allan Poe. Kaplan wondered if they were on the trail of Poe, or if Poe was on their trail. He wondered about the missing manuscript and if they would run into Poe again. One year later, Kaplan would get his answer.

On Sunday, April 13, 1980, the Kaplans found themselves leading a parapsychological study group from Pennsylvania on a psychic tour of New York. They had chosen the sites carefully. First they visited Robert Fulton's grave in lower Manhattan; there the psychics among them were told by the ghost of Robert Fulton that the car of the future, in the next twenty to thirty years, would have only three wheels.

Then they went to Queens to visit the residence of the master of magic and illusion, Eric Weiss, alias Harry Houdini. Houdini rests in his family's plot in Machpelah Cemetery in Glendale, Queens. The group held the largest formal séance ever recorded there: more than thirty-five people formed one large séance circle.

After the séance, the group piled into their privately chartered bus for a drive to the Bronx and the former home of Edgar Allan Poe.

It seems they were expected.

They traveled up the Grand Concourse, toward Fordham Road, and arrived outside the cottage, located in Poe Park, on East Kingsbridge Road. Many years ago that area had been a part of Westchester County, not New York City, and the original cottage had been moved a block or more during the construction of the Fordham Road area. But the cottage and all the furniture were Poe's.

The group passed through a large metal fence surrounding the wooden cottage that Poe and his wife, Virginia, had rented in 1846. Virginia Poe had died the following year of tuberculosis in the small bedroom of the cottage.

In the entranceway, the group was given a brief lecture by a guide and then allowed to roam through the house. As Kaplan walked around, he started to feel a presence, a familiar presence. Was Poe still trying to contact them? He asked his wife, Roxanne, to take pictures of everything in the hope there might be a clue as to what was going on.

At the end of the tour the Kaplans wished the Pennsylvania group well, and drove to their home in Elmhurst. The next day they took the rolls of film to be developed, and counted the days until the prints could be retrieved.

As the Kaplans looked carefully at each picture for quality and clarity, they hoped that one of the photographs might reveal some clue as to the strange feelings Kaplan had experienced. Could a camera see something that the human eye could not?

And then they saw it. One picture taken in the Poe sitting room showed a rocking chair, surrounded by a light mist. It could have been anything—poor developing, even a reflection of some sort. But the other pictures showed no sign of photographic error.

Several weeks later the Kaplans were visiting radio and television broadcaster Joel Martin and his wife, Christina, in Long Island. Since 1974 Kaplan had been a frequent guest on Martin's shows, telling fans about his exploits in the mysterious world of parapsychology and the occult.

The two men were going over the pictures that had been taken during some of the Kaplans' various trips, when they came upon the sitting-room picture. Kaplan's mouth fell open in shock. The picture was different. The mist had changed.

The amorphous mist surrounding the chair had more form, had solidified—and an image, faint yet new, had appeared. The Kaplans looked at the picture again and again. What had happened?

A *Ghost Forevermore*

Could a photograph capture a real spirit or ghost in the same way legends claimed it could capture a living person's soul or spirit? If so, could a picture, once developed, continue to "further develop"? The four knew that it was impossible. Yet something had happened, and was happening, but what?

Kaplan carefully removed the sitting-room picture from the rest of the photographs and placed it in a single envelope. He wondered whether, if they waited another week or more, they might see how the picture would further develop. They left the photograph with the Martins; that way, the Kaplans could not be accused of tampering with the picture.

It was hard to wait the week, impossible to wait more. Excitedly the Kaplans went back to the Martins' home the next week. Kaplan carefully took out the photograph, placing his fingers on the edges so that his fingerprints would not be on the picture.

Now each of them—Joel, Chris, Roxanne, and Stephen—viewed the sitting-room picture, carefully passing it from person to person.

The hazy shape had indeed become more focused. There was a person sitting in that rocker. And that person looked like someone whose picture the Kaplans had seen before, in old portraits and drawings. It was the author of "The Tell-Tale Heart," "The Cask of Amontillado," and "The Red Mask," the man who had become famous for stories showing how the living cannot escape the dead. It was Edgar Allan Poe. He appeared to be smiling at the group as he sat in his wife's favorite chair.

The picture remains in the possession of the Parapsychology Institute of America. Some people who have examined the picture claim that the form sitting in the rocking chair changes from time to time. They say they can sometimes see Virginia Clemm Poe.

Could it be that Edgar Allan Poe leaves the picture for a while to visit some of his favorite haunts? He did, after all, live in a great many places. Does he return for a while, after searching for his lost manuscript? Or is he restlessly partaking of his persistent addictions, even though they eventually killed him?

Whatever reason Poe's spirit finds to roam the earth, some part of that spirit remains with the living: he is eternally rocking in a rocking chair, not only in a cottage in the Bronx, New York, but in a carefully guarded photograph. Forevermore.

Chicago's Most Haunted Cemetery

Dale Kaczmarek is the head of the Ghost Research Society and editor of the Ghost Trackers *newsletter. He has been actively investigating paranormal phenomena since 1975 and he personally conducts tours of legendary haunted areas in and around Chicago. He works with psychics, not only in Illinois but out-of-state as well, in investigating "ghost lights," haunted houses, battlefields, and cemeteries.*

His activities have been written up in magazines and newspapers and he has appeared on television and radio shows from California to Vancouver. Though his case files are stuffed with unusual stories, one of his favorites is about a century-old cemetery, long abandoned, which has been the site of incredibly diverse supernatural activity—all of it terrifying. . . .

Near Chicago's Rubio Woods is a haunted and long-forgotten cemetery called Bachelor's Grove. Generally, graveyards are not the best places in the world to look for ghosts, since they prefer to haunt the place where they met their deaths. Still, the dead do not rest easy here and, as a result, there are many old legends about the cemetery.

One such tale concerns a strange ghost known as the "Hooked Spirit" because on one arm he has a hook

51

instead of a hand. It is said that he likes to sneak up on couples in parked cars. He is sometimes reported to be carrying a double-barreled shotgun and chases these lovers from the property which once belonged to him.

In one version of this story, a young man parks in the Bachelor's Grove area and tells the story of the Hooked Spirit to his girlfriend, hoping she will melt in his strong arms for protection. Instead, she is frightened and asks to be driven home.

When they arrive at the girl's house, the young man gets out of the car and walks around to the girl's side to open the door for her. He gets the shock of his life when he finds a hook still swinging on the door handle. Apparently they left the area at the right time, because the Hooked Spirit was just about to open the car door when they pulled away, ripping the hook from his arm!

In another old and well-known legend, a couple is parked near the area, again engaged in amorous activities, when suddenly they hear a frightening report over the radio. A mass murderer has escaped from a nearby psychiatric hospital and was last seen heading in their general direction.

The girl is scared and demands to be driven home immediately. However, on this occasion the car will not start. The young man tells the girl to stay in the car and lock the doors and windows while he goes to a nearby service station for help.

He is gone for quite a long time, and during his absence she hears a strange scratching sound coming from the roof of the car. She just shrugs it off as the branches of nearby trees.

Finally she sees the blinking red and blue lights of the local police as they pull up to the disabled car. She is quite relieved and opens the door to greet the friendly and most welcome faces. A policeman orders her to continue walking toward him and not look back under any circumstances. She finds that a bit strange, but obeys his command. As more and more squad cars arrive and begin shining their spotlights in the direction of her car, curiosity gets the better of her and she turns around.

She shrieks in sheer terror as she sees the bloody body of her boyfriend hanging upside down from a tree directly above the roof of the car. His throat has been slit from ear to ear and it was his fingernails making the scratching sound on the roof.

It's not known how or why these legends began, but as horrifying as they are, they are like comic-book versions of what really happens in Bachelor's Grove.

The cemetery's uneasy history begins in the nineteenth century, when the area was originally settled about 1830 by a group of predominantly German immigrants. They helped dig the old Illinois-Michigan Canal and later built small homesteads in the huge groves of virgin timber, while perfecting their titles to tracts of land they purchased at $1.25 per acre. Each man had a five-acre woodlot in the grove, and the settlement was known as Bachelor's Grove because of the large number of unmarried men. The Grove was on the northwest corner of the township, on 143rd Street, just east of Ridgeland Avenue.

The immigrants also set aside a graveyard for their dead. The first legal title on record was in 1864, when Edward Everden sold his land to Frederick Schmidt; one acre was set aside for the graveyard, which remains to this day. Burials continued until 1965, which is the last official grave marker. After that, the site was abandoned as a graveyard because of increased vandalism and grave desecrations. Gravestones were defaced with graffiti and spray paint. Sometimes tombstones were stolen, only to be returned later. In 1964 and 1975, graves were dug up, the caskets broken open, and the gruesome contents strewn about. Not even the presence of Cook County forest rangers deters the vandals.

Near a lagoon, in one corner of the cemetery, the remains of small animals and chickens have been found, all decapitated and totally drained of blood. In 1974 and 1975, forest rangers who patrolled the woods at night would come across this gruesome evidence of voodoo rites and devil worship. Around them, the rangers saw inscriptions on the trees and rocks: strange occult symbols that were spray-painted in red. Some of the symbols can still be seen today.

Once, the cemetery was easily reached by 143rd Street, which runs directly in front of it, but the road was later abandoned when the Midlothian Turnpike was built nearby. So not only did the decades pass it by, but so did modern technology. Now the cemetery is overgrown with weeds, and although it is surrounded by an eight-foot-high Cyclone fence, entrance is gained by slipping through one of the holes cut into the fence by vandals or through the broken main gates.

Upon entering the cemetery, one of the first things that one notices is the total lack of animals within the cemetery boundaries. There is plenty of fauna both visible and audible just outside the chain-link fence, but not within. It is literally devoid of life!

However, consider what happened to two young women on two separate occasions in August 1984, during the cycle of the full moon. While visiting the cemetery in the evening, two friends experienced cold, sweaty hands and the impression that someone was following them, someone not of this world! They also heard strange voices coming from the direction of a small grave near the front fence and saw a nebulous white form in the immediate area. They described the area as being considerably colder than the surrounding area, and the inside of the cemetery appeared to be lit up in some strange manner. At first they thought that their minds or eyes were playing tricks on them, but the same thing happened two days later during another visit!

A few hundred feet from the cemetery is the small lagoon, which is fed by a small creek flowing through the woods. The lagoon can be seen by motorists passing by on the Midlothian Turnpike. It looks tranquil and harmless, but the legends associated with it are quite terrifying. Its horrific background dates from the 1870's, when a farmer and his horse were plowing some land right by the lagoon. Suddenly, without warning, the horse bolted toward the small body of water with an incredible strength, taking with it the farmer and his plow. The farmer couldn't swim, the horse was hindered by the weight of the plow, and both drowned.

Several years ago, while on car patrol late at night, two Cook County forest rangers suddenly saw a ghostly apparition emerge from the lagoon—an old man with a horse pulling a plow. The apparition crossed rapidly through their headlights and then vanished as the rangers reached the opposite side of the Midlothian Turnpike at Rubio Woods. The men just stared at each other in total disbelief. At the time, they decided not to officially report what they'd seen for fear of ridicule and being passed over for promotion.

During the Roaring Twenties and into the 1930's, the lagoon was a favorite dumping ground for gangsters. Many bodies were found floating there. With such violent deaths over the years, one would expect the lagoon to be haunted . . . and it is—but not by something human.

People walking in the woods and even motorists on the turnpike have sworn that a bizarre apparition crawls in and out of the lagoon. Late one night an elderly couple was traveling along the turnpike, returning home from a party. As they approached the small stone bridge that spans the creek which feeds the lagoon, they noticed a movement just under the bridge. Suddenly the awesome figure of a two-headed man strode out from under the bridge and crossed in front of their headlights before mysteriously vanishing in nearby Rubio Woods. Needless to say, they stepped on the accelerator and made it home in record time!

The street where this weird apparition was reported is a hotbed of other strange reports as well. The Midlothian Turnpike (or 143rd Street, as it is still sometimes called) recently has been the scene of disappearing cars.

On several occasions, witnesses have reported seeing what appeared to be a car or truck suddenly disappear with apparently no place to go! The stories are similar: the people are traveling in a westerly direction on the turnpike when they see what appears to be the red taillights of an automobile not too far in front of them. As they apply the brakes to slow down a bit, just to be careful, they suddenly see the brake lights go on.

They usually assume that the car is a police vehicle or forest ranger, pulling into one of the park entrances to set up some form of speed trap for unwary dragsters. As they approach the area where the car appears to have turned off, they can find no trace of an automobile. In fact, in all instances, a chain is blocking the park entrance and the phantom car is nowhere in sight!

Other times the lights actually have been attached to phantom cars and pickup trucks; motorists, driving down the turnpike, drive alongside a car and then pass it, only to see the entire car disappear in their rearview mirrors.

In another, more eerie encounter, two men were passing the area just before reaching the small stone bridge. It was an hour before dusk. As they approached the bridge, the front-seat passenger noticed a dark silhouette as large as a full-size car parked on the right shoulder. He kept his eye on the car just to be sure that a door wouldn't suddenly open onto the road. When the men passed the dark shape, the passenger looked in the outside mirror, only to see no car or silhouette shape visible! It had suddenly disappeared!

In a similar incident, a few blocks farther east, near the intersection of 143rd and Central Avenue, a single woman driver had a most unusual event take place.

It was a warm summer evening, around 9:30 P.M. The car windows were rolled down so that she could enjoy the gentle breezes and fragrant smells of the nearby forest preserves. She drove north on Central Avenue and came to a stop at the stop sign at 143rd Street. She was very careful to yield to all oncoming vehicles in the immediate area because there had been a number of serious high-speed accidents in the area in the preceding months.

After stopping, she pulled out and made a right turn onto what appeared to be a clear roadway. Suddenly she noticed a gray blur of an automobile, with no lights on, coming fast from her left-hand side.

She quickly slammed on the brakes but felt a thud on her front fender—but she saw no vehicle that could have caused the impact. She even got out of her car and looked up and down the street but could find no trace of an automobile, nor of any skid marks. There was no damage to her car, but plenty of damage to her nerves as she quickly sped from the scene.

And just down the street from the road to Bachelor's Grove, a young South Side couple smashed into a phantom sedan. They had stopped their car at the intersection of Central Avenue and the Midlothian Turnpike and were looking both ways to make sure it was safe to go. They had just made sure no other cars were in sight, and the way was clear, and had pulled out into the street. Suddenly a brown sedan came out of nowhere, speeding toward the cemetery. The young man driving the car hit his brakes. But it was too late. As the brakes screeched, the two cars hit with a sickening thud, and the couple could hear the crash of dented metal and breaking glass. Dazed, they looked up, only to see the brown sedan fade away. When they got out of their car to survey the damage, their car was totally unmarked.

In most cases, when phantom cars have been reported, there was past evidence of a murder or abduction resulting in murder near the scene. However, there are no such events connected to the Bachelor's Grove area. These phantom cars will undoubtedly continue to baffle and elude motorists in the area for some time to come.

As you leave the modern turnpike and turn into a small dirt trail, you actually enter another world almost 160 years old. This small trail is known as Bachelor's Grove Road and is the original roadway used by the early pioneers, long before the more modern concrete highway was built. It is along this now unused roadway—blocked off by chains, "No Trespassing" signs and concrete pillars—that you will find Bachelor's Grove Cemetery. Almost a quarter of a mile into the woods, the forgotten burial ground is located.

From the cemetery, proceeding west, the road has been almost completely reclaimed by the forest-preserve vegetation. Further exploration beyond this point locates the road leading to Ridgeland Avenue. From that point to 147th Street and Oak Park Avenue, once known as Goeselville, no signs of the road seem to exist.

However, looking west-southwest, one can still see evidence that a road once continued further. In fact, it ended near what is now Harlem Avenue and approximately 150th Street. Near this point, a school once stood, called Bachelor's Grove School.

The road itself has been the scene of inexplicable phenomena from time to time, including a fiery red "skyrocket" effect which has been seen whizzing up and down the main trail. At first it was assumed the lights were the result of simple pranks by neighborhood teenagers shooting Roman candles or bottle rockets up the trail from the other end.

However, this phantom red skyrocket comes out of nowhere, zooms up and down the main dirt path leading to the graveyard, and leaves a red trail in its wake. The red light is so brilliant, and the movement so quick, that it is difficult to tell what the object really is. And as if to tease the terrified viewer, the rocket likes to fly down the trail, stop, hover, and zoom back—over and over again, in rapid succession. Similar bizarre skyrocket effects have often been recorded in UFO reports.

The most famous "ghost-lights" story connected with the cemetery itself is the many, many reports of strange blue balls of light seen bobbing around the graves—apparently with some intelligent control. In other words, they elude pursuit.

A man from Joliet, Illinois, reportedly chased these strange lights on at least two occasions. Each time he saw one, it changed in size and grew as large as a basketball. It flew around the cemetery with lightning speed, blinking at ten- to twenty-second intervals.

As he attempted to approach the light close up, it suddenly faded from view and then reappeared behind him at approximately the same location where he had first encountered it. This feature repeated itself over and over again throughout the time he observed the phenomena.

In December 1971 the light was seen by a young woman who was able to reach out and touch it. She put her hand right through the light, as though nothing was there. She claimed to have felt nothing at all, no heat, no cold. This is highly unusual among reports involving ghost lights, however.

To this day, she is the only person who has gotten close enough to the light to touch it. Usually the light acts as if it is wary, weaving and bobbing away from outstretched hands, and moving in the opposite direction of anyone who follows it.

Another man encountered the light in 1975 with a group of his friends. At first he thought it was simply a trick of the eyes, or the sun reflecting off something shiny, like a metal sign. He described the light as "deep blue" and visible from the opposite end of the main trail after he and his group became "spooked" by it! It was observed as high as tree level on that particular occasion.

Other people have described "a feeling of something huge and alive," as large as thirty feet square. While the shape of the blue light varies with each observation, an obscure object thirty-by-thirty would be an immense and quite frightening thing to behold!

Almost all ghost lights elude pursuit and even become invisible if the observer does not maintain the proper viewing distance. Some lights react to both lights and sounds and may suddenly split up or disappear rapidly if approached with bright lights or with loud noises. This is the case in Bachelor's Grove, with one important exception: this light has been seen in broad daylight.

Ghost lights are not uncommon throughout the United States, and have been reported as long ago as the 1800's—long before automobiles that could have caused such lights. Yet that is the standard theory for many ghost lights. However, Bachelor's Grove is not the only cemetery in the United States which has been the site of strange blue lights. A small cemetery in Silver Cliff, Colorado, has been plagued with the same blue balls of light appearing in it for several decades. It was even investigated by the National Geographic Society!

Perhaps the most startling and interesting story connected with the main trail surrounds a phantom farmhouse which appears and disappears alongside the road. These reports date back to the mid-1950's and the farmhouse is still being sighted today—in many cases by people who do not know of the Bachelor's Grove legends.

This phantom house is definitely not a trick of the eye and it is not caused by the trees and foliage combining to give the viewer a false image of a house. This has been reported in all weather conditions and during the daylight and evening hours as well.

There is no evidence in any historical records to indicate that any such farmhouse, or any other building, for that matter, ever existed on either side of the road at any time in the Grove's history! The phantom house apparently moves about from one area to another. Sometimes it's reported on one particular side; other times it has moved to the opposite edge of the roadway. When Dale Kaczmarek, of the Ghost Research Society, personally interviewed witnesses and asked them to mark an X on a map of the area, the witnesses marked X's all over the map!

However, he has found that the description of the house remains constant. It's always described in exactly the same manner: a white farmhouse with white wooden pillars, a porch swing, and a light burning faintly in a window. But as the house is approached by witnesses, it appears to shrink, to get smaller and smaller until the image itself disappears from sight. No one has ever made it to the front steps of the house, and perhaps that is fortunate. Given the way the house vanishes at will, those who would set foot on the wooden porch might also vanish from the face of the earth.

Disappearing houses fit in with the theory of a possible interdimensional doorway existing somewhere in the region. The area can remain dormant for a good number of months, up to a year, and then suddenly a completely new rash of sightings will crop up. The phenomena are constantly changing and are always new and diverse.

There have been apparitions and ghosts reported within the area. A ghost is a form, shape, mist, or shadow that does not have identifiable form or configuration to it, while an apparition appears to be either a person, or animal, or inanimate object because of its recognizable form or shape. Some apparitions even have clear facial features as well.

The two most frequently encountered apparitions within the Grove are strange monklike figures and a woman carrying a baby.

Perhaps the moving house is the origin of the "Madonna of Bachelor's Grove." This ghostly figure of a woman, sometimes carrying a baby in her arms, is seen roaming the cemetery at night. She is seen only on moonlit nights and only when there is a full moon.

She is also known as the White Lady. No one knows her story or why she is doomed to spend eternity at Bachelor's Grove. She appears to simply wander aimlessly through the cemetery, with no apparent direction in mind. She is not aware of her human observers, or else just doesn't care. These encounters are always quite short but very impressive.

To add a little fuel to the fire, there is a very small grave in Bachelor's Grove with the simple inscription "Infant Daughter." Makes you wonder, doesn't it?

Two young men had some very interesting encounters to report after they visited the area one evening. As one wandered through the cemetery, he saw flickers of light darting continually through the flora. He thought the lights were being reflected off of something, but he could find nothing to account for them. There was no object in the vicinity to reflect light. As he turned around rather abruptly, he still swears to this day that he saw what can only be described as a black dog whose rear end faded away into nothingness.

His friend claims that he heard a distinct voice mumbling a word over and over again, coming from a distance but sounding right near his ear. He never could make out the word, but the voice was described as extremely sensual, almost sexual.

Norman Basile, a paranormal investigator in the Chicago area, has been to Bachelor's Grove many times. He says that walking down the cemetery path is like stepping into a freezer, even in the summertime. In 1983 he felt a presence near the entrance and took a photograph in the direction of the "feeling." When developed, the picture showed a bluish mist with a face in the middle of it! That same year, he took his family on a tour of the cemetery. His mother called out in alarm, and the entire family ran to her side. She was standing and looking at a tombstone—they all saw it— which bore a ghostly face. As they stared at it, the face slowly disappeared.

In 1984 Basile and a friend tried camping out in the cemetery for the night—and never made it. They arrived at ten P.M., carrying camera equipment and special microphones. For a few hours, nothing happened; then, suddenly, everything happened at once. Basile and his partner were standing back-to-back (presumably to avoid having something sneak up on them) when the friend cried:

"Oh, my God! Look what's standing over there by the trees!"

By the time Basile turned around, the apparition had disappeared. His friend saw a man, in his forties, wearing a suit and a hat—only he was all yellow.

Then they saw the red streaking lights, and watched in disbelief as a single tree began to shake frantically. All the other trees stood perfectly still. By that time, Basile's friend had gathered up an armful of equipment and was running toward the car. The evening was over.

Other sightings in Bachelor's Grove include matched descriptions of the figure of a small child running across the bridge from one side of the lagoon to the other and the sudden appearance of a huge cathedral-size church in a large blank section of the cemetery. Could this be another varied description of the phantom house that so many other people have seen? Or is this perhaps yet another strange sighting to add to the list?

Several people have reported seeing a black carriage being drawn across the lagoon toward them. Could this sighting be associated with the apparitions of the farmer and his horse?

There are also stories of a strange monklike figure, not only in Bachelor's Grove. This sight is a persistent recurrence throughout the Chicago area and constantly shows up at locations where there was never a history of a monastery. The other possibility is that these "phantom monks" are simply people dressed for cult activities or black-magic rituals who were mistaken for ghosts. The last reported encounter with a ghostly monk was in the early 1980's.

Ghost researcher Dale Kaczmarek thinks he may have uncovered some clues. He was investigating the cemetery in 1979 and took a series of photographs at random, including one of the fence surrounding the cemetery. When it was developed, the picture showed a black-hooded figure standing in front of the fence.

The figure was dressed in monk's robes and held a baby in its arms. Dale took the photo three years before he had ever heard of the "Madonna of Bachelor's

Grove." Other photos, taken with high-speed infrared film, show floating faces, high above the chain-link fence surrounding the cemetery.

Other researchers have captured unwanted images on film too. In 1975 one man went to the Grove with an SX-70 camera—and the camera began to take pictures by itself! When developed, the photos showed a large blue-gray mist hovering over the entire area—a mist the photographer hadn't seen. He brought his camera to the experts at Kodak, who pronounced it in perfect operating condition.

A student at De Paul University took a series of infrared photographs. The resulting pictures showed horrible red demonic faces on various tombstones, in the trees, down the paths, and in the lagoon.

Norman Basile has taken many photographs. Faces show up on tombstones, ghostly forms stroll down paths, odd lights bob up in unexpected places, and the blue mist continues to flow—all captured on film.

Some of Dale Kaczmarek's photographs show a number of reddish streaks that appeared out of nowhere. When he took the photos, Kaczmarek saw nothing that could have caused the red lines, but it makes sense to think he may have captured on film the ghostly vapor of the red rocket.

Because of the abundance of paranormal encounters and strange phenomena that hundreds of people have seen, heard, or felt, Kaczmarek felt that Bachelor's Grove needed a professional psychic. On May 1, 1982, he put together an investigative team that included himself, his brother Wayne, and Pat Shanley (not her real name), a professional psychic healer and noted clairvoyant. Shanley is also a reader, ghost investigator, healer, teacher, and lecturer. She has been hired to find missing people, lost belongings, and, on occasion, murderers.

True Tales of the Unknown

At that time Pat Shanley was a member of an Illinois society for psychic research. Dale first met Pat when he was asked to lecture at the society. His subject was spirit photography, and after the lecture Pat approached him with the idea of working together for a time conducting ghost research. He agreed and thought that the perfect starting point would be Bachelor's Grove Cemetery.

They arrived there on a bright, sunny afternoon with high hopes of capturing something on film and perhaps sorting out some of the mysteries associated with the place. They used various types of equipment, including a video camera, in case anything unusual would be visible to the naked eye, and a portable tape recorder to document Pat's impressions and Dale's note-taking. Also employed were two thirty-five-millimeter SLR cameras on separate tripods with individual cable releases. One camera was loaded with high-speed infrared color-slide film, which was pushed to four hundred ASA, and the other camera was used as a control to document the infrared and was equipped with ordinary color-slide film.

As they first entered the cemetery, they felt nothing out of the ordinary . . . until they arrived at the large Fulton tombstone, which is the largest such marker in the entire graveyard. The front face of the marker is a curiosity, as it's only half complete. One side is ornately and beautifully carved with swirls and spirals. The other is still a rough block of granite which was never started. On occasion, photographs of the Fulton tombstone have revealed monstrous faces.

They stopped near the tombstone to allow Dale to set up his equipment, and he began recording what Pat described:

"I see something that keeps switching between this hideous-looking animal and a man dressed in strange-looking clothes. He has a lot of money. He won't say what he did. Something very wrong."

As she is describing this, another entity enters the picture, and Pat continues:

"The little girl is his daughter, who is now a young woman."

"What style of clothing does he have? What era can you pick up?" Dale asked.

"He looks to me like a cross between a saloon keeper and an Irish dancer," Pat said. "He's got a loud, clashy-looking vest on. Strange-looking derby and a gold watch. He feels very guilty about something and cannot even leave this area. He complains that he's fenced in because of his deeds. I have to assume from what I have seen that there was a black iron grille fence here and he feels that because of what he did, he has to stay within this perimeter. I told him that he doesn't have to."

"Can you pick up any names?"

"When you said that, the name John came to my mind."

Pat was correct in that Fulton's first name was John. John Sr. emigrated from Ireland in the 1830's to this area and his son John Jr. was also buried here with his father. Dale wondered which John this might be.

"John might have been the man that he committed the terrible offense against," Pat continued. "I believe that it might have been someone in his family. His daughter is not an infant anymore. She looks like she's about seven years old now. She could leave. He feels he can't."

"Is he dominating her?" asked Dale.

"Yes, but she was standing over here"—Pat indicated an area between a small tree and the large tombstone—"and trying to hide from someone. He was very bold and standing right out in the open. I don't get the impression of murder, but he did something that was terribly wrong. It had to do with money. I don't know why he sometimes takes on the form of an animal, snarling and growling."

"Is the daughter shy?"

"Yes, but she may be shy because she's had no real contact with a lot of people, but she's had contact with this snarling man. I get the name Ann for her. I'm sure that's correct. I also see a group of about thirty people over here."

Pat pointed to an area just to the left of the Fulton tombstone and close to the lagoon. She turned toward the large group of people, who were invisible to Dale.

"How are they dressed? Same era?"

"I don't know," Pat replied. "I was just aware that they were there. I'll have to go into trance to see exactly what they look like."

She paused for a few moments while she prepared to go deeper into a trancelike state. In such a state, Pat could pick up even more detail and actually communicate with entities on the other side.

"This may be a wagon and a horse," Pat began, "that fell into the water somehow. These people, I think, don't have anything to do with that action."

"How are they dressed?"

"These people aren't dressed in any one time period, and they would not be seen in their dated clothing. They are more inclined to be wearing robes. The main complaint among them is that they must stay here." She paused for a minute or more before continuing, "The reason that they must stay here is that no one has taken them away. Some of these clothes could be dated. I don't think any are earlier than the 1890's. But they are really later than that. I would say between the twenties and the forties is the time frame when most of these people died."

"Do you feel that the people you are seeing were buried in this cemetery?"

"Yes. Definitely. But I don't know—they're not Germans, though. They're not all Germans."

"Do they know each other?"

"Oh, yes, definitely by this time!"

"Are there more men or women?"

"It's about evenly distributed," Pat responded, "and there are children here too. When looking at this, it almost makes me wonder about the idea that I had: a certain aspect of man cannot ever leave the earth, and these people are bound here for some reason until a certain time has passed. Then they are taken away."

"Do you pick up any names at all?"

"Strange name like Dorma or Dora. Dora Myers. The wagon that I see does not fit; I remember now what you said about a farmer and his horse. What I am looking at does not look like a plow or a flatbed wagon. It looks more like a carriage. I think you said it was a farmer?"

"A farmer and a plow," Dale responded.

"What I see is a man in a carriage. Now, why it would change, I don't know. He did fall into the water, but I believe that these things have the ability to change their appearance. In other words, I think that if he didn't like showing himself dressed up like a farmer, he could make himself appear to look more prosperous and have a carriage instead of a plow."

"These people you see," Dale pressed, "they're on this side of the fence?"

"Yes."

"Where do you pick up the most of them? By the trees there?"

"Do you see this tree right in the middle?" Pat asked. "They're more grouped in front of it. They're sort of wandering around aimlessly, in a suspended state. There is a baker here saying, 'You shouldn't be doing this.'"

"Is he dressed in a baker's outfit?"

"Yes. In fact, he even has a rolling pin in his hand."

"Did you pick up these people as we first walked in?"

"I just knew that they were there," she said. "I wasn't trying to pick up anything at that point. I have never just sat down and done this in a cemetery, though I once did this at a funeral in the cemetery, where I saw the person who had died. I never expected to go to a cemetery and find people hanging out in one special area. The peculiar thing is that the man doesn't leave that area."

Suddenly Pat turned quickly to the left. Apparently she spotted another image in a more remote part of the cemetery.

"There's a woman over there that won't leave that area as well. Though I don't think she's the occupant of the grave. She looks sort of angelic. She might not even be a woman. She wants to talk about something, I don't know what. There's a nice white glow around that area, also. It extends about four feet high and three feet wide."

They slowly walked toward the glowing area, where there was a tombstone. As they bent down to read the inscription, Pat said the name aloud.

"Her name is Meyers."

Dale was astounded. Pat had picked up the name telepathically before they actually arrived at the grave marker. She couldn't have picked up the name telepathically from Dale, because he only knew the family-plot marker name as Newman. She was listed on the tombstone under her maiden name of Meyers.

"Do you think that this might have been the Dora that you picked up before?"

"I'll find out when I go into trance. She had been calling me over here. She wanted to talk to me, more than the other spirit that's here. He couldn't care less. He is not very friendly."

Just about this time a group of Cub Scouts came out of the woods from a nearby trail. Apparently out hiking with their scoutmaster, they must have entered the cemetery while Dale and Pat were still in the process of their investigation. The first odd thing that they noticed was that all the scouts went directly to the large Fulton tombstone first, even though there were other large tombstones they had to pass before reaching the Fulton marker, which is on the far side of the cemetery from the hiking trails. Dale asked Pat if the ghosts were still there. He asked her to watch the ghosts' reaction to the newcomers, while Dale would observe any curious actions by any of the scouts or the scoutmaster.

"Is she still there as well?" he asked.

"She tried to get away, fade away. The scoutmaster walked right on her feet.... Now the other entity—the man—is snarling at me and looks kind of beastly."

"Is it actually a human form that you are seeing?"

"It changes. It's pretty sad. What I originally saw was a monk with a doglike face. But then when I asked him to reveal himself as he was, what I saw was this man."

"Do you feel that he revealed his true self to you?" Dale asked.

"He seemed very conceited, really. I suspect that's what he really looked like. He was sort of a chubby man, somewhat rotund. Small, about five-five."

After the scouts left the area, Dale and Pat turned their attention back to the Newman/Meyers tombstone.

"This light that I see ... I'm not sure that that has anything to do with her. There are two different kinds of phenomena here," Pat said as she entered into a somewhat deeper trance. "She can go back and forth. She's waiting for her children to die. She says that her husband is no longer here, so she's alone, waiting. I told her she's waiting for nothing."

"Maybe her husband moved on?"

"Yes, that's what she said. Now, that's the first one that I've heard say that. That sort of discounts my theory that they *have* to stay here. She looks very happy, very content. Yet she says that staying here is a form of self-punishment. In other words, they are staying here because they want to. It's a sickness, to a certain extent, to want to stay in a cemetery."

"How do you account for the glow? Is that associated with her or is it another phenomenon?"

"I believe that's another person," Pat stated. "It may be a father. There is definitely a person in that grave. They're very highly involved. Now, why would the energy stay there? Perhaps the energy was so great from that person that they have left some kind of imprint there."

"Is she the Dora that you picked up before?"

"Yes. In other words, she was over there, and when we came over here, she followed us."

They decided to rest for a bit here, and this gave Dale the opportunity to ask Pat some general questions regarding her clairvoyant ability.

"What do you actually pick up when you go into trance?"

"When touching things, I can pick up images, vibrations, which usually start telepathic pictures going. First of all I look for heat to tell me that something's there. The tombstone is less helpful than the ground."

"Do you ever get a numbing sensation?"

"Yes, it's like my hands are tingling."

So Pat is able to pick up telepathic and clairvoyant images by simply touching items, as many psychometrists do. But that same ability is not just limited to psychometry, because she is also able to see these images while not in physical contact with anything. This way she can also analyze and question the being or entity at will.

Dale and Pat made a complete round of the cemetery and now approached the front gates, pausing beneath some evergreens. Suddenly Pat saw yet another image of a person standing near the front fence.

"Again I see an energy field here, but it's not that strong. It was stronger, very strangely, when those kids were here. . . . Something's standing right by your cameras."

"On which side?"

"Right behind the camera, when I first looked at it."

"Did it seem to notice the camera equipment?"

"Yes."

"Let me try something. Let me move the cameras back and see if it follows them." Dale moved the cameras closer to the front gates. "Is it still here?"

"Yes. It's right behind the camera, on the right side. It's definitely interested in the cameras. I'll go into trance so I can communicate with it."

Pat prepared herself for another trancelike communication session. "He wants us to take his picture. He's straightening his hair. He looks like a farmer. He looks about sixty. He doesn't like the sound of that, because he thinks he's very handsome. He says he died of a heart attack."

"Why does he stay?"

"Strange answer . . ." Pat mused. "He says, 'I have no place to go.' He's very tanned. His hair is almost completely white. He's very interested in our mechanical age. He says it's a shame that nobody comes back here with those machines anymore."

It was late in the afternoon, on that May 1, 1982, when they ended their investigation near the main gates.

The video camera was used sparingly and no paranormal images were captured or observed on the replays. Besides the conversation between Pat and Dale, the only other sound recorded on the portable tape recorders was the drone of jets soaring overhead.

No paranormal voices or noises were detected on playback.

During that afternoon, they had used a half-roll of film in both the infrared and control cameras. They finished the other half during a different investigation at an apartment on Chicago's South Side. A few weeks later, they saw the puzzling results.

When the film was retrieved, Dale and Pat noticed that all the color infrared film taken that afternoon in Bachelor's Grove was completely washed out, even though the control film—shot at the same speed, lens opening, and at the same instant—came out perfectly normal. It couldn't simply be bad film because the second half of the infrared film taken at the South Side apartment building was normal in both color and exposure.

Apparently someone or something that afternoon at Bachelor's Grove Cemetery did not want itself seen.

Pat's impressions, on several instances, matched recorded events and encounters reported by other reliable witnesses. Other impressions were later documented and verified through research and fact-finding excursions.

On a subsequent follow-up investigation, done several months later, very little in the way of psychic phenomena or psychic impressions was felt by either Pat or Dale. One possible explanation is that the original visitation was made shortly after Walpurgis Night— the night when ghosts and the spirits of darkness roam the land. It gets its name from St. Walpurga, who is regarded as the protector of humanity against evil magic.

Those of you who may want to visit the area and conduct your own psychic investigations should arrive there in the morning or afternoon. Evening investigations are not appreciated by the local authorities, and you could well find yourself in jail for trespassing.

However, the place is easy to locate when traveling west on the Midlothian Turnpike (143rd Street) from Cicero Avenue toward Ridgeland. When you see the Rubio Woods Forest Preserve, park your car there and carefully cross the turnpike. There you will find a small unused dirt trail leading to the cemetery, about half a mile into the woods. Just follow that trail to its end.

You can't miss it, unless, of course, the ghosts have moved it again.

The Screaming Child

Professor Gene Snyder has spent the last fifteen years teaching a course called Literature of the Occult at Brookdale Community College in New Jersey. More than thirteen hundred students have taken this course, with many staying on through the second term, which focuses on the actual field investigation of the paranormal.

Snyder and his students have a hands-on approach: they personally visit each location and carry out a complete investigation, using many kinds of techniques, from science to psychics. Perhaps the strangest and best-documented of such cases occurred not far from the college in a comfortable middle-class suburb. (Other than Snyder, all the names have been changed.)

It's hard to believe that a new tract house—that looks just like the other row houses—can be haunted. But it was....

Tom and Corey Hampton were the proud owners of their first house, a Colonial in the twenty-year-old tract in the Oak Hill section of Middletown, New Jersey. They were both New York City commuters and, as Tom's career as an investment banker was doing very well, they bought the large house on more than a half-acre of ground in anticipation of starting a family.

The Hamptons felt that their real-estate agent had gotten them a tremendous "deal" on the house. It appeared that the seller had been suddenly transferred to a Midwest location and had been forced to sell well below the fast-escalating market price. The Hamptons moved in in the late fall of 1979 and started to redecorate.

They were in the house less than a month when the nightmare started.

They were still tired from the Thanksgiving holiday. After a tiring drive for dinner with Tom's parents, he and Corey returned late, leaving the car in the driveway, as the garage was still full of unopened boxes. The next day they dragged themselves out of bed and spent the long weekend unpacking. Each night they fell into bed exhausted.

At two in the morning on the night of November 28, Corey was awakened by a noise from the downstairs portion of the house. As the Hamptons were new to the suburbs and newer still to the house, Corey dismissed what she heard and Tom continued to sleep soundly beside her. She'd always remarked that it would take a bomb to wake Tom. By contrast, she had always been something of a light sleeper.

She listened for a long moment, trying to remember exactly what the noise had been—it sounded like a child crying. Dismissing it, she went back to sleep.

It was less than a half-hour later when she was again awakened by another sound. This time it lasted longer, and Corey was fully awake for a period of eight to ten seconds before it stopped. It *was* the sound of a child crying. She was certain of it. She was equally certain the sound was coming from the rear downstairs portion of the house. The back part of the house had an unusual building configuration. The back of the Colonial, normally perfectly flat, as were the others in the tract, had been changed by a former owner. He had created an extension for the first floor which had enlarged the house by some five and a half feet by seven and a fraction feet. It was a mudroom and it was one of the few things that set this particular house off from the others on the block. As close as Corey could figure, without getting out of bed, the sound was coming from that area. After a minute or two, the crying stopped.

Corey was not a woman prone to flights of fancy. She was calm and levelheaded, with a bachelor's degree in finance and a management position with a mortgage company. As she started to relax, she dismissed the thought that the sound had been her imagination. Imaginary sounds did not awaken one from sleep. There were times that nightmares did wake her up, but this was not one of them. There *was* a sound, and it *did* seem to be a child crying. It least it was a familiar sound—a lot more reassuring than the sound of a burglar breaking in. On that note, she went back to sleep.

Over coffee the following morning, Corey asked Tom if he had heard anything during the night. As expected, Tom said he had heard nothing. Following their usual schedule, she and Tom got ready for work. As they drove down the street, Corey saw Mrs. Angistino, her next-door neighbor, waiting at the school-bus stop with a little girl of five or six. Perhaps the neighbor's child had been crying and there had been some trick of sound—the strong northwest wind, possibly—that had made the noise "feel" as if it had been coming from the mudroom. That answer satisfied her . . . at least until the following night.

It was close to two A.M. when Corey was again awakened. There was a violent rainstorm outside and the positioning of the house atop a small rise, somewhat exposed to the elements, provided no protection from the northwest wind that had grown to near-gale force.

Corey was sure that it was the whistling of the wind and nothing else that had awakened her. It was as noisy tonight as it had been deathly silent the night before. Still, there seemed to be another sound in the wind. It was a keening wail that could have been a product of the interaction of gusting wind and some corner of the roof or drain gutters. She tried to separate the alien sound from the creaks and gusts.

After a moment, a particularly strong blast of wind awakened Tom, who sat up, surprised to see Corey awake.

"Do you hear it?" she asked.

"Do I hear it? It woke me up . . . and I just don't normally wake up. Hell of a wind."

"No. I mean the other sound."

"What other sound? How could you hear anything else but that hurricane out there? I better check the doors and windows."

Ever the careful new homeowner, Tom got up and pulled on a robe. Corey listened as he walked down the hall and the stairs. Again she tried to find the strange wailing in the wind. She couldn't detect it. After a few minutes Tom came back to bed. Aside from a few broken limbs in the backyard, there was nothing he could see that was amiss.

The next morning dawned clear and chilly. Both Tom and Corey had the day off from work. They spent a portion of the morning clearing the limbs that had been blown down in the backyard. While working near the property line, Corey saw Mrs. Angistino doing the same thing in her yard. Her little girl, Karen, was playing on a jungle gym. The two struck up a conversation about the storm. Angie Angistino grumbled that her husband hadn't managed to get the day off as he'd planned. He worked for the power company, and he had been called out at six in the morning to work on downed lines from the storm.

After a few minutes the topic turned to children. Angie Angistino said how nice the neighborhood was for raising children. Without any thought at all, Corey found herself asking a question.

"Did Karen have a nightmare the other night?"

Angie looked confused. "No. Not that she mentioned. Why do you ask?"

"Oh, I guess it's just being new to the house. I woke up in the middle of the night and thought I heard a child crying. It was quite intense."

"From our house?"

"Well, not actually. It sounded more like it was coming from the downstairs of our house." Corey shrugged. "If it wasn't Karen, perhaps it was the house settling or something in the heating system."

"I guess so. You two don't have any children in the house...not yet, anyway." Angie's tone had become strained, or at least that was what Corey seemed to perceive.

"Well, I better get Karen back inside before she turns into an icicle." Angie smiled and headed off to her daughter.

It was close to 2:30 the following morning when Corey again awoke with a sudden start and a shiver. She could hear a raucous buzz that even woke Tom. After a second of listening, he jumped from the bed and grabbed his robe.

"Smoke alarm...downstairs. Get something on," he yelled as he headed out of the bedroom in the direction of the stairs.

Corey was only seconds behind him as they dashed down the stairs. Tom was snapping on lights as he went and, as far as Corey could see, there was no smoke anywhere. When they got to the smoke alarm near the kitchen door, the sound suddenly stopped.

They stood there staring at one another for a long minute. Tom took a dining-room chair, stood on it, and removed the smoke alarm to check the batteries. Perhaps it was the type of alarm which sounded when the batteries were low. But the batteries were fine.

The smoke alarm had been only two or three feet from the arched doorway that led to the mudroom. Leaving the disassembled smoke alarm on the kitchen table, Tom checked the stove, oven, and gas heater in the basement to ensure that they were off, that there were no gas leaks or pilot-light outages, and that everything seemed to be working properly. It was, so they returned to bed.

Corey considered telling him about the sound of the child crying but thought better of it. She had a hard time getting back to sleep and it was about an hour later when she finally drifted off. Tom, as usual, had gone right back to sleep.

She estimated that she was asleep for less than a half-hour when a sound again awakened her and Tom. It was not the smoke alarm, and there was little or no wind. This was the terrified scream of a child—coming from the mudroom.

Through her shock and fear, Corey also felt relief. Tom had heard it too.

"What the hell is that?" he bellowed.

As he spoke, the scream stopped, as if suddenly choked off, and an eerie silence fell over the house. Now it would be Tom who could not get back to sleep. Padding around in his slippers and robe, he looked through the house from the basement to the crawl-space attic. After about forty minutes he came back to bed shaking his head.

Corey knew that the search was more Tom blowing off steam than anything else. She debated telling him about what she thought the "noise," as he called it, sounded like. But both of them were totally rational people, Tom even more than she. The thought of anything metaphysical or supernatural was something totally out of their ken; something for the front pages of supermarket tabloids. However, Corey decided to take the risk of upsetting Tom.

"What do you think it sounded like?" she asked.

"It sounded like a cat caught in machinery," he grunted.

"No, it sounded like a child . . . screaming." She waited for his reaction before she went on.

"Maybe." He shrugged.

"This isn't the first time I've heard it. It's just the loudest."

She told him about the previous two nights and even about asking Mrs. Angistino if Karen had been having a bad dream.

"The noise seems to happen the same time each night, and it gets . . . I don't know . . . more desperate each night."

"Next you're going to say that the house is haunted."

She put an arm around his shoulder. "I don't believe in that stuff. That only happens in the movies."

The next night was Saturday and they both stayed up late watching a movie on television. By the time they went to bed it was nearly two and Corey made sure that she stayed awake for a time, lying there listening. There was neither a cry, nor a scream, nor anything that could be called out-of-the-ordinary. Satisfied, Corey went to sleep.

The sound did not come back, and within a month they had all but forgotten about it. Tom had replaced the smoke-alarm battery, even though the old one had tested out at full charge. Generally, their lives moved past the event as if it had been a ripple in a slow-moving stream.

It was during the week between Christmas and New Year's that the sound began again. The pattern was identical. The sound started about two in the morning and increased in severity or intensity from the first night to the third.

On the first night, Corey awakened Tom after listening to the sound for a few minutes, and Tom, as was his habit, donned slippers and robe and sped downstairs to the kitchen, only to find that, as he approached the mudroom, the sound stopped. On the second night, Tom waited up, and when the crying sound started, he snapped on a tape recorder. Later, he discovered that the sound did not appear on the tape. It made no sense at all. If they were hearing "it," whatever "it" was, then its sound should record on tape.

On the fourth night the sound stopped, as it had the month before. It seemed that it appeared, in increasing severity and volume, only on or about the last three nights of the month.

Corey had always been something of a problem-solver. She was a woman who enjoyed reacting to challenges, and she was not going to attack this problem any differently from the problems on her job. Because she knew nothing about the supernatural, research was the answer.

The Middletown Public Library was one of the better-stocked libraries in the county. Corey spent several evenings there researching material about the supernatural, ghosts, hauntings, and anything else that might relate to the sound of the "screaming child," as she had started to think of it. When she exhausted the local library's supply, she moved on to the eastern branch of the Monmouth County Library. It was there one evening that she saw a familiar face as she looked through the stacks.

It was Angie Angistino. As it happened, they were both looking for material on the supernatural. Angie indicated that it was for a course she was taking at the local community college, a course called Literature of the Occult.

"They give courses in such things?" Corey asked in surprise.

Angie explained that in fact she was taking the second semester of the course and that it was fascinating. She was researching a paper on the supernatural for a presentation in class. As Corey seemed very interested, Angie invited her to come to the class and sit in, assuming that the professor wouldn't mind.

The following Thursday night, Corey met Professor Gene Snyder. He was a tall, serious-looking man with a graying beard and an infectious laugh. He called the students by their first names and generally seemed to know what he was doing. Corey had learned from Angie that he had spent years researching the paranormal. He was a parapsychologist and a researcher of all things unusual. His classes were fully accredited college-level courses that dealt with unusual material.

There were three student presentations in the evening, and a question-and-answer period followed each. One was on UFO's, another was on Zen meditation, and the third was on reincarnation and something called the "near-death experience." By the end of the evening, part of Corey was fascinated and part of her was sure that this was the stuff of *The National Enquirer*. It was only after Angie introduced Corey to Professor Snyder and the two got a chance to speak for a few minutes that Corey realized he and his students were dead serious.

"Sounds like you've got a ghost," he said nonchalantly after she explained the events at the end of November and December.

Corey was appalled. "You make it sound so commonplace."

"It's more common than you think. But somehow, discussion of the supernatural is often limited to such places as a class like this. People feel if they mention it to anyone they will be considered crackpots and social pariahs. When Angie first mentioned this course, I'll bet your first reaction was something like, 'They teach courses like that?' "

Corey burst into laughter and then stopped herself. "I'm sorry, Dr. Snyder, I—"

"Don't worry about it. These courses have been running for something over five years. I've heard every reaction I think I could hear."

She explained more about the events, and he listened, nodding as she spoke.

"Yup. Sounds like you need someone to do a Holzer-type investigation, but that will take some time. Perhaps there are some students in the class who would be willing to take it on. It can serve two purposes that way. They can use it in the course and, perhaps, get you some help in making sense of it."

"Can you . . . they get rid of it?"

"I have no idea. That depends on what 'it' is." Professor Snyder also told Corey to bring her husband to the next class meeting. "You're going to need his cooperation and support in this matter."

Getting Tom to come to a meeting was a project in itself. He refused and made fun of the whole thing.

"This clown is a college professor and teaches things about ghosts? What kind of college is that, anyway? And what kind of character is this guy?"

Corey explained what she had researched of the professor's background: "He's got three college degrees, is a combat-decorated Vietnam veteran, and he's published lots of books. Sounds to me like he's qualified. Besides, he runs a darn good class. I know. I sat in. And I hesitated at first too."

Tom flatly refused. He considered the entire idea nonsense. Corey could find no way, short of starting an enormous fight, to get him to cooperate. She went to the following meeting of Professor Snyder's class with Angie and again spoke to Snyder afterward.

He listened thoughtfully before he spoke.

"It normally doesn't do much good in cases like this to push too hard. Your husband's reaction is called 'cognitive dissonance resolution.'"

"Cog what?"

"That's a mouthful, isn't it? Basically, it means that he has a set way of seeing the world. Most of us do. When something comes along which he accepts as real but which, at the same time, contravenes his world view, he will react in a disruptive way. You see, you either have to discredit what you *know* you witnessed or you have to change your world view. The former tends to be the more popular reaction."

"You mentioned a name when we spoke last . . . and connected that to an investigation?"

"Probably Holzer."

"Yes. That's the one."

"That's Dr. Hans Holzer," Snyder said, identifying Holzer as a renowned parapsychologist who had spent many years researching and writing on ghosts and hauntings. "Generally, he considers that a ghost is a displaced soul, lost and clinging to the last place it lived."

"Why does that happen?" Corey was astonished to hear herself. A month earlier she could not have conceived of asking such a question or of sitting in on the class at all.

"We don't know. I think that's the phrase I have used most with my students over the years. There are a lot of things we don't know. Holzer gives us a procedure, though. It's a form of investigation that he uses in such cases. I'm afraid there's a bit of legwork to be done. There's also the need for some observation of the site of the occurrence. That was why I was hoping you could get the cooperation of your husband. If both of you are interested in a solution, then my team turning up at the house would not be an intrusion."

Corey decided to ask Tom again. But over the next few weeks she never seemed to find the right time. It was on a Friday night near the end of the month that she found she did not have to be very persuasive. Events would overtake Tom Hampton.

It was on the last three days of the month of February when the sound came back again. Either it was louder and more plaintive or both Tom and Corey were especially attuned to it. On the third night, the twenty-eighth, two in the morning again brought forth screams that made Corey pull a pillow over her head. It was a child in absolute terror, or one being tortured.

Tom dashed downstairs and headed to the kitchen. As he snapped on the kitchen light, the smoke alarm wailed and, as quickly, went silent. The scream was still there and Tom approached the door to the mudroom. Corey had come downstairs a minute or so behind him. As he reached for the doorknob he could almost feel the child scream. The sound was deafening. Corey wondered if the neighbors might hear it.

Tom grabbed the doorknob and as suddenly let go.

"It's hot!" he yelled.

"Don't touch it again. There might be a fire in the mudroom."

Tom didn't listen. He braced himself against the door and again reached for the knob. He quickly turned it and eased the door open.

The knob was now cool. The screaming stopped. The mudroom was empty.

The following Thursday Tom joined Corey in Professor Snyder's class.

Snyder explained to them that there had to be a game plan in any investigation. He also warned them that to find the root of the problem was not an assurance that the disturbance would disappear. Tom haltingly agreed to an investigation.

Since Snyder's previous talks with Corey had all been brief and somewhat hurried, he arranged to meet the couple for coffee at a local diner. He had to interview them about the specifics involved in such an investigation.

A few days later, he and the Hamptons sat in a booth for an hour of coffee and conversation. Snyder turned to Tom.

"Did you ever think this might have had something to do with the bargain price that you paid for the house?"

Tom scratched his head. "Who would have thought that? I mean, who in his right mind . . . ?" He stopped and managed a sheepish smile.

"By extension indicating that those of us who investigate such phenomena are not quite in our right minds. No offense taken. Most people who have this problem are caught up between a belief-structure rock and a hard place. How old is this tract in Oak Hill?"

Corey answered. It was she who had done much of the research on the house before they purchased it.

"It was built in the late fifties. Fifty-eight, as I remember."

"I assume you had a survey and title search done?"

They nodded.

"Well, you're going to have to go to the Hall of Records in Freehold and look back through the chain of ownership on the property. Records on Middletown are pretty good, as I remember. What you're looking for are structures that were near the present one."

Tom shook his head. He still had a hard time being part of such a bizarre event, let alone taking part in a ghost hunt. "Dr. Snyder, I'm sure you know what you're doing, but what does this have to do with the 'thing' that turns up at the end of every month?"

"It's part of Holzer's theory, and a number of others have written about it. When we see this kind of manifestation, it's usually in an 'old' place. Ghosts don't move, you see. They seem to be caught up in a loop that periodically moves them from wherever else they exist back to here. They don't seem to know that time has passed."

"Okay," Tom said. "I think I can understand that . . . not that I can say I completely believe it. But why are they in the loop, as you call it?"

Corey smiled. Perhaps Tom was finally warming to the idea of a supernatural search. She felt that he had started to join her in the solving of a problem.

"There's just speculation on that," Snyder said. "One possibility is that they were caught up in the middle of an action that was crucial when they died, and they seem compelled to complete the action. Another is that they died suddenly, often violently, and their personalities are held together by the conviction that they are not dead. Generally, they seem to be as frightened of us as we are of them.

"But the first thing to do is check the history of the property. Then you'll have to find a substrate map of the area to look for any geological faults. In addition, it's a good idea to see if you are in line of sight of any microwave transmitters. You know, the ones that transmit cable signals."

"Whoa!" Tom said with a laugh. "Too fast. What does that have to do with all of this?"

"There is a chance that the manifestation is completely conventional. Something could be causing the effect that has nothing to do with the metaphysical. As I told your wife, there is some legwork to be done here. There are two of my students who are willing to do some of the work for you so that they can do a presentation on the research. They're both interested in researching ghosts. It's an opportunity for them and a bit of help for you. I'll give them your phone number, if you wish."

Corey nodded; Tom shrugged. He was still not completely convinced.

As they were about to leave, Tom asked a parting question. "What kinds of conventional things?"

"Let me give you an example," Snyder said as he pulled on his coat.

"There was a farmer in Iowa about ten years ago. He started to wake up in the middle of the night hearing voices... music and other strange sounds. His wife and children didn't hear them. He was the only one who did. Also, he did not hear them anywhere but in the bedroom of his house, usually in the middle of the night. After a month of sleeplessness the man started to see a psychiatrist twice a week. He had had six months' worth of very expensive therapy when, as suddenly as the sounds had started, they stopped. The normal thought would be that he was unbalanced and that the therapy got to the root of things. It was wrong.

"The man had gotten some dental work done in the same time period that he was hearing the sounds. The silver amalgam in his fillings was acting as a receiver for a radio signal emanating from a leak in a transmitter tower of a local radio station. When the station corrected the signal, the sounds stopped. A counterpart of mine in the Midwest came up with that. He saved the man's peace of mind and a great deal of money spent in more therapy. You have to check that kind of thing out before you start to consider the supernatural."

Tom laughed. "Weird as that story is, it makes more sense to me than ghosts."

In the next three weeks, Tom and Corey, along with Alma Benziger and her sister Mary, two of Professor Snyder's students, researched the property as best they could. There were no microwave or radio signals. There were no ham radio operators in the area. There were no geological faults. But it was in the property records that they started to find interesting data.

The tract had originally been a farm that had been parceled off and sold to a developer. The farm owners, a family named Hockson, had traced their ownership of the property back to the post-World War I years. They had built a farmhouse on approximately the same spot as the existing Hampton house. But there was nothing in the history of the Hockson family to account for a screaming child. They would have to search further. Hopefully they would find something more tangible before the end of the month.

On the night of the twenty-seventh of March, in the teeth of a gale that had blown in a large snowstorm, the sounds returned. The next morning, Corey phoned Professor Snyder.

"It's back."

"Both of you heard it?"

"Loud and clear, about two in the morning. Even though I've done a lot of work on this, it's still scary. I'm yawning at my desk today. Tom and I were up for several hours last night."

"I'll call the Benzigers and see if we can put a recorder in that mudroom of yours."

It was eight in the evening when Alma and Mary Benziger arrived to set up the tape. They used a large Ampex tape machine requisitioned from the college and ten-inch tape reels that would be set to record very slowly. One reel would last from ten in the evening to six in the morning, so that the tape machine could be left unattended and no one would be required to get up in the middle of the night to turn the tape over. Alma also used an omnidirectional microphone, which simulates the human ear. It was about nine in the evening when Professor Snyder stopped by to check the setup.

"You know," said Corey, "Tom and I tried recording this sound once before, with no luck. Is there anything else we should do?"

"No. As a former audio engineer, I can tell you that the kind of recorder used, or the speed of the tape, has nothing to do with the frequency level of a supernatural sound. Sounds, even supernatural ones, will be recorded; in fact, it's unusual *not* to record them. A recording is useful evidence. But it isn't something that will get rid of your visitor."

Corey found his remarks disquieting. What *would* get rid of whatever it was?

Close to two o'clock in the morning, the sound started again. It was somehow clearer, and started as a whimpering, then became a crying. Corey clung to Tom in the bedroom. She was not afraid; she had become used to the arrival and departure of the sound. She could only feel a great sadness. It was the cry of a child—a child who had become lost and for whom they could do little.

The cry grew more urgent and Corey found herself crying as it rose to a terrified scream. Tom held her and they forced themselves to wait it out. Professor Snyder had asked them to do that. He was hoping to find exactly when the sound stopped by itself. Each time it had occurred before, Tom had managed to stop it by his intervention.

It was twenty after two when the sound suddenly stopped. By three, Tom and Corey had managed to go to sleep, exhausted and drained.

In the morning, Alma Benziger arrived to retrieve the tape and the machine. Three times she played the section of tape that had recorded during the time of the sound. There was nothing on it—only air noise from the amplifier being turned up to maximum gain.

In the days that followed, Snyder had the tape listened to by a professional audio engineer. They rerecorded it at a faster speed, for clarity. Although there were a few odd areas on the tape, mostly there was silence. He exposed the recording segment to an oscilloscope. There was not a waver on the screen. The machine had recorded nothing outside normal parameters.

It was two weeks later when Alma Benziger called and said she had managed to unearth some material that the Hamptons might find interesting. The two sisters, along with Professor Snyder, met with Tom and Corey in the living room of the Hampton home the following night. Snyder had read the file that Alma had found.

"It seems," he said, "that the Hocksons bought the farm from the Underfelds, another family of farmers, in 1911. The Underfelds had owned the farm from around the turn of the century. The Underfelds' house had been on the same lot as yours, but not in the same spot as your house. It was positioned so that the front of their farmhouse was close to what is now the rear of your house.

"On the night of"—Snyder paused and looked to a copy of a battered newspaper clipping from the local newspaper of the time, called the *Middletowner*— "November 30, 1911, there was a fire in the Underfeld house. It seems an oil heater tipped over in the basement near the front of the building. All of the family managed to escape except for the youngest son, Jesse. He was a boy of seven. He was somehow trapped under the stairwell of the front stairs. He burned to death there."

A silence fell over the group as Snyder paused.

Corey spread her hands in a gesture that was both helplessness and curiosity.

"Then what we are hearing is Jesse crying to get out?"

Snyder nodded slowly. "It would seem so. What you are hearing happens at the end of every month, corresponding to when the child died. Oh, and the location of the stairwell is significant too."

"Why?" Tom asked.

"It exactly corresponds to the position of your mudroom."

93

Tom Hampton was not happy with this explanation. He was even more unhappy over the next four months when Professor Snyder had two psychics come to the house. Snyder thought the two psychics might persuade the troubled spirit of Jesse Underfeld to leave.

The first psychic, an older woman, walked through the entire house, up and down the stairs, and into every nook and cranny. But she felt nothing. The second psychic, also a woman, but younger, did sense an enormous amount of pain in the mudroom. But she announced that she wasn't able to do anything about it.

Corey considered calling in a clergyman; Professor Snyder said that sometimes that had worked in the past. The clergyman would tell the spirit that it was dead and order it to go to its rest... and perhaps the spirit would heed.

But after this last discussion, Professor Snyder never heard from the Hamptons again. He didn't know if Corey and Tom ever went to a clergyman, but he felt Tom Hampton probably reverted to his cognitive dissonance resolution. But coincidentally, Snyder was friendly with Louise Tyler, the real-estate agent who had originally handled the sale of the Hampton house. And in the spring, Snyder learned from Louise that the Hamptons put the house on the market, pricing it below market value. It was sold in the summer. Two years later it was sold again... and again. Professor Snyder did not ask if they ever told the buyers about the screaming child. He didn't have to.

As a result, the Colonial tract house seems to have a permanent "for-sale" sign in front of it. If you drive through Middletown and spot a house at a bargain price, think twice before you buy....

The Brown Mountain Lights

Michael A. Frizzell, of the Enigma Project, has been investigating strange phenomena for nearly two decades. He has seen many unusual and mysterious things over the years, but the one that fascinates him the most is the Brown Mountain Lights of North Carolina.

The lights have been seen for a hundred years, perhaps longer. Curiosity-seekers and scientists alike have tried to explain them away, but they are still there. . . .

The Blue Ridge Mountains are among the oldest peaks on earth, having been geologically dated at nearly 2.5 billion years. At the end of the mountain chain, about fifteen miles north of the town of Morganton, North Carolina, sit Brown Mountain and its nearest neighbor, Chestnut Mountain. Brown Mountain is so badly eroded that its elevation now barely crests 2,700 feet. Composed almost entirely of cranberry granite, in geological terms, Brown Mountain is not much to get excited about. However, persistent stories of its mysterious lights do give pause for thought.

The "Brown Mountain Lights" have often been described as intense, multicolored point sources of light seen on and about Brown and Chestnut mountains in western North Carolina. The lights are said to exhibit limited lateral and horizontal movements during some of their occasional appearances. A few witnesses have even claimed incidents of rare "close encounters," in which they described the lights as fifteen-inch balls of yellow or blue-white fire that emitted sizzling noises.

Theories on the origin of the lights have run from the ridiculous to the sublime. From such baseless ideas as swamp gas and uranium deposits to the more sophisticated, tenable notions of earthquake lights, many concepts have been proposed, but none have been proved. Folklore, too, has had its romantic say in the matter—with the lights being caused by the disembodied spirits of, variously, a brutally murdered housewife, young lovers who expired during a Brown Mountain tryst, and the lost souls of countless Cherokee braves who died in battles fought hundreds of years before the white men came.

However, there is just as much conjecture over what causes the lights as there is concerning when they were first reported. The earliest published account of the lights appeared in the Charlotte *Daily Observer* as a dispatch from Linville Falls, dated September 23, 1913. The article credits the actual discovery of the lights to members of the Morganton Fishing Club, who claimed to have first observed the lights' nocturnal wanderings about 1909. The late Joseph Loven once reported that he first noticed the Brown Mountain Lights as early as 1897, when he moved to Cold Springs, a community very close to Brown Mountain. Earlier still, Colonel Wade H. Harris, a former editor of the Charlotte *Daily Observer*, stated in a letter dated October 2, 1921, addressed to former North Carolina Senator Simmons, that "there is a record that it [the light] has puzzled the people since and before the days of the Civil War."

In any event, persistent sightings of the Brown Mountain Lights during the first decade of this century aroused the first "official" study of the phenomenon. As a direct consequence of those early sightings, North Carolina Representative E. Y. Webb urgently requested an investigation of the lights by the United States government. In response to Webb's request, D. B. Sterrett, a member of the U.S. Geological Survey, was sent to Brown Mountain on October 11, 1913 to observe the lights and determine their origin.

Presumably Sterrett arrived at Brown Mountain with no preconceived notions on the lights' origin. After spending several evenings examining the oddity, he concluded that the strange lights were undoubtedly caused by the refraction of locomotive headlights straying from certain peaks beyond Brown Mountain. Local residents were skeptical. Sterrett's theory was just a little too simple. In fact, Sterrett's locomotive theory lost all its steam with locals during the great flood of 1916, when virtually all trains operating within a fifty-mile radius of Brown Mountain were put out of service for almost two weeks. According to newspaper accounts, the Brown Mountain Lights continued their nocturnal antics during that time.

A more extensive written account of the lights appeared in a news article for the Morganton *News Herald* on December 16, 1915. Joseph Loven, C. L. Wilson of Lenoir, North Carolina, and another friend set up a vigil in Morganton in the late afternoon. About 6:45 P.M., while the three of them were crouched behind a knoll to shield themselves from the wind, Loven suddenly said, "There's the light."

"That's a skyrocket," Wilson replied. At the south end of the mountain, seemingly near Joy Post Office, was a light resembling the morning star or a discharge from a skyrocket.

From that time until eight P.M., for a duration of one hour and fifteen minutes, the men watched the light. It appeared fifteen times at different points; it was in view for only one-half minute each time.

The men felt the light had no resemblance to the reflection from a headlight, but had characteristics all its own. It also reminded them of a person, at some distance, carrying a lighted lantern and moving around with about the speed of a balloon. C. L. Wilson "did not regard it as a weird light, yet I noticed I did not sleep quite so well after viewing it as I do at home."

On April 11, 1916, H. C. Martin and Dr. L. H. Coffey of Lenoir organized an expedition to investigate the Brown Mountain Lights. Martin's party set up their operations on Adam's Mountain, a peak closely neighboring Brown Mountain. Their observations for the evening were largely uneventful until 11:52 P.M. At that time Martin saw two floating spheres of light, "apparently about the size of ordinary streetlamps of Lenoir seen from a distance of about one mile." Martin reported that the lights flashed out among the trees on the eastern slopes of Brown Mountain about one-eighth of the distance down from the summit. The lights moved southeasterly, in a roughly horizontal plan, floating in and out of ravines and generally following the contour of the land for a distance Martin estimated at two miles. The lights accomplished their trek in twenty-one minutes. According to Martin, at 12:13 A.M. they disappeared as abruptly as they had come.

In the year 1919, Professor W. G. Perry of Atlanta's Georgia Polytechnic Institute had been so intrigued by stories of the lights that he journeyed to the area to examine the oddity firsthand. In a letter addressed to Dr. C. G. Abbott of the Smithsonian Institution, dated December 15 of the same year, Perry described the lights as he saw them from the area of Cold Springs:

"We occupied a position on a high ridge. Across several intervening ridges rose Brown Mountain, some eight miles away. After sunset we began to watch in the Brown Mountain direction. Suddenly there blazed in the sky, apparently above the mountain, near one end of it, a steadily glowing ball of light. It appeared to be about ten degrees above the upper line of the mountain, blazed with a steady yellow light, lasted about half a minute, and then abruptly disappeared. It is not unlike the 'star' from a bursting skyrocket or Roman candle, though brighter."

The seekers of conventional explanations have suggested that Martin's luminous anomalies, and other cases paralleling his account, were individuals walking the slopes of the mountain with lanterns. Superficially this sounds plausible. But it is not possible. Martin said his mysterious globes of light traversed the slopes of Brown Mountain in twenty-one minutes and covered an estimated distance of two miles. If his figures are reasonably accurate, this would equate to a speed of 5.7 miles per hour. For many individuals, on level pavement, jogging at such a speed would be no great athletic accomplishment. However, Brown Mountain has a sixty-degree grade, and is covered with rocks, ravines, vines, and "rhododendron hells." A typical rhododendron bears little resemblance to those found in the wilderness areas of North Carolina's Pisgah National Forest. "Rhododendron hells" are eight- to ten-foot-high wild flowering rhododendron shrubs that stretch for many acres. These woody shrubs are many decades old and often form mazelike tangles which folklore credits as causing madness in hikers. The suggestion of a lantern-carrying jogger negotiating such difficult terrain strains credulity.

In 1921 the more boisterous spectators again wrote to North Carolina Senators Simmons and Overman to obtain another (and hopefully more acceptable) study of the enigma. This time the U.S. Geological Survey dispatched George Rogers Mansfield to head the investigation. Mansfield arrived on the scene in March 1922. He spent two weeks in the immediate vicinity of Brown

Mountain and made observations of the lights on seven evenings from a variety of vantage points. He conducted interviews with witnesses claiming familiarity with the phenomenon and carefully documented all of his telescopic and photographic measurements. He concluded his investigation with a very scientific and comprehensive report entitled *Origin of the Brown Mountain Lights in North Carolina.*

Unlike Sterrett, Mansfield attempted to cover all bases, for he assigned not one cause for the lights but four separate causes. He summarily indicated that 47 percent of the lights were caused by automobile headlights, attributed 33 percent to locomotive headlights, 10 percent to stationary lights (houses and other structures), and finally, 10 percent to brush fires. Possibly Mansfield arrived at the above conclusions because he was categorically studying common misinterpretations of the "true" Brown Mountain Lights. It is entirely possible that Mansfield never saw the real anomaly, or if he did, he may have mistakenly factored it into his percentage groups.

Sadly, as a result of Mansfield's report, there was a significant lack of interest in the lights from about 1926 until the early 1960's, with little new documentation.

In the summer of 1962, three Morganton-area businessmen, Paul Rose, Howard Freeman, and R. M. Lineberger, spearheaded a special project which would provide superior photography of the lights and possibly yield an answer to the mystery. They constructed a fifty-foot observation tower near Brown Mountain's summit. Essentially, they intended to monitor the lights when they appeared on nearby slopes. Their efforts seemed wasted, mainly because of bad weather, until one evening when several project members were "buzzed" by a sizzling ball of fire while standing in the tower. Afterward, several of them experienced dizziness and nausea as a result of the incident. Shortly after this encounter the project was disbanded. The fifty-foot wooden tower was apparently dismantled long ago; Michael A. Frizzell, research director for the Enigma Project, a Maryland-based phenomena-research association, has made yearly trips to the area and has never been able to locate it.

Frizzell is a research technician and analytical chemist. Along with Bob Lazzara, he co-founded the Enigma Project in 1978 and has been actively investigating and researching claims of unexplained phenomena for over seventeen years.

Frizzell first became acquainted with the Brown Mountain Lights in 1968. An *Argosy* magazine article called them "perennial unidentified flying objects." Being particularly enthusiastic about UFO's, Frizzell found the idea of being able to visit a "flying-saucer" hotspot an appealing prospect indeed. Just imagine, one specific location you could visit, almost anytime, to observe UFO landings and departures! It wasn't until 1974, however, that he first went there in person. In 1978 he embarked on what would become a four-year study of the Brown Mountain Lights with the Enigma Project.

Frizzell made an impromptu trip on Saturday, October 12, 1974, when he was living in Marietta, Georgia. Along with his friend Steve Benson (not his real name) he drove five hours to the Route 181 overlook, an area only 3.5 statute miles west of Brown Mountain, which affords a panorama of that mountain and a great many miles of lower elevation beyond it to the east.

Frizzell and Benson were remarkably unprepared for this adventure, neither one of them possessing or having access to a 35mm camera (110 Instamatics and Polaroids were useless, as they cannot take time exposures). Other than a portable shortwave radio, which they used to receive accurate time signals (from WWV in Colorado), they had no special equipment.

They arrived at the overlook around five P.M. and set up an observation post on the state-built graveled parking area; it provided a magnificent unobstructed view of

Brown and Chestnut mountains. During their entire vigil, Frizzell and Benson made all their observations while perched atop a large rock that sat within the overlook's parking area. The weather was cool and clear, typical of a fall day in the mountains.

By 6:30 P.M. darkness had set in and Frizzell trained his full concentration on the not-so-lofty peaks. As he watched and waited, a slight mist veiled the mountains. Nevertheless, the objects of his attention were still sufficiently visible. Just as he began to question the horse sense of the five-hour drive to the area, a tantalizingly brief but intense flash of white light appeared among the trees on Chestnut Mountain's northern slope. Whatever misgivings he had had were now squelched and the adrenaline was flowing.

During the ninety minutes that followed, Frizzell became the captive audience of a most unique light show. Although he never saw more than four or five lights at any one time, by the end of the display he would see about forty lights in all. All the lights originated below the crests of Brown and Chestnut mountains. Those that did appear took on a variety of colors. Their general appearance, viewed at a three-mile distance, was similar to a welder's arc in brilliance, with their initial color being blue-white or yellow, tapering off to a dull red before extinguishing. They seemed to wink at him from the mountains' deepest recesses.

His excitement ran so high it was difficult to remain calm and objective about what he was seeing. But during the entire sighting, Frizzell was able to sketch everything they saw and write accurate minute-by-minute notes of their observations.

Some of the lights exhibited a wavering horizontal movement of about two or three degrees. All the lights accomplished their color changes and lateral maneuvers within the brief span of two to ten seconds. By eight

P.M. the activity had all but ceased and a dense fog enveloped the mountains, calling a halt to any additional observations. As Frizzell got into his car and drove away, the kaleidoscopic display he had witnessed was rushing through his mind. Benson was decidedly skeptical, but Frizzell never ceased to wonder what the lights were.

In May 1977, an investigation of the Brown Mountain Lights was conducted by the Oak Ridge Isochronous Observation Network (ORION), a UFO-research organization based in Tennessee. ORION wanted to explore the hypothesis that the refraction of distant city lights could possibly be misinterpretations of the true Brown Mountain phenomenon. One evening ORION researchers strategically placed a group of observers at the Route 181 overlook, three-and-a-half miles west of Brown Mountain, which gives a panoramic view of the mountain and a great many miles beyond it. At the same time, in Lenoir, a town located twenty-two miles east of Brown Mountain, ORION members positioned a 500,000-candlepower arc light facing the Route 181 overlook to the west. Brown Mountain was now between the town and the overlook. When the light was turned on, its characteristically brilliant blue-white beam was observed at the overlook as a strange orange-red orb apparently hovering several degrees above Brown Mountain's crest.

The experiment proved that many past reports of the Brown Mountain Lights—manifesting themselves above the mountain's crest—were, in all likelihood, light refractions emanating from some point beyond Brown Mountain and only appearing to be immediately above it. Therefore, in the majority of cases where the lights had been observed as being above the mountain's crest, it was likely that the reports were merely cases of mistaken identity. Nevertheless, beyond this majority of cases, the true Brown Mountain enigma then consists of only sightings of the lights on the mountain among the trees, both at a distance and up close.

Lights typically seen above the mountain can probably be dismissed as an optical deception attributable to refraction, but this does not explain what Frizzell, and countless others before him, saw on the mountain. Little did Frizzell know at the time that this, his first sighting of the lights, would be the most outstanding spectacle he would ever see. Had he been better prepared at the time, today he might be much closer to an explanation for these mysterious lights. Since 1978 he has made at least fourteen separate trips to see the lights, with each trip consisting of no less than three days.

Unfortunately, these odd lights are most frequently spotted at inconvenient distances of three miles or more. Logically, if Frizzell was to study these distant objects in greater detail, somehow he had to get closer to them.

In an effort to make some reason out of the Brown Mountain rhyme, the Enigma Project joined forces with ORION in 1978. Researchers from both groups began to take a hard look at the anomaly to better determine scientific methods of studying it. The first joint Enigma/ORION venture occurred during the first week of July 1978.

Approximately twenty researchers converged on Brown Mountain with cameras, telescopes, magnetometers, communications gear, and Geiger counters. Among the participants were two chemists, a physicist, a mathematician, two electronic engineers, a chemical engineer, and an electronic assembly technician. With gear poised, they strained their eyes every evening of that week, getting no reward for their vigilance.

Then one evening toward the end of their stay, they were gifted with a significant sighting. At precisely twelve midnight a bright, diffused white light appeared among the trees on the northern slopes of Chestnut Mountain. Although they did not photograph the light, it performed a five-second horizontal zigzag movement before blinking out. They did, however, manage to measure the length of the movement within the five-second interval. Based on their three-mile distance from the mountain, they determined that the light's approximate speed was fifty-five feet per second (37.5 mph). Considering that particular velocity in such rugged terrain, devoid of all but the most primitive roads, they discounted any manmade contrivance as being the cause of the strange light.

All their machinery showed no extraordinary activity. And the Geiger counters showed normal background activity. They were not able to come to any conclusions about the origins of the lights. Four other joint trips took place from 1980 to 1984. The participants in each of these ventures basically remained the same; however, on two of these trips, George Walls (an engineering manager and Enigma Project engineering director), Bob Lazzara (an industrial-engineering manager and Enigma Project operations director), and John Cooper (chemical engineer and Enigma Project field investigator) were also present.

One of the many researchers was a Maryland resident prior to 1981. However, after participating in one excursion early in 1981, she became so enthralled with the Brown Mountain region that she permanently relocated there. She is still there and has become a most reliable and tireless researcher of the Brown Mountain Lights phenomenon.

As a longtime researcher of the Brown Mountain enigma, Frizzell admits that while he doesn't know exactly what the lights are, after having observed them firsthand, he most confidently knows what they are not.

He seriously doubts that the Brown Mountain Lights are UFO's. They aren't any form of technological hardware, extraterrestrial or otherwise. As for the rest of it . . .

Many theories have been advanced on the nature and origin of the Brown Mountain Lights. Refractions of manmade lights account for a large portion of these sightings. It is even possible that the mysterious lights Frizzell observed showed color changes because of refraction (*i.e.*, mist around the mountain).

Swamp gas is invariably a tired stock explanation for many near-ground-level nocturnal lights. Where Brown Mountain is concerned, the swamp theory does not seem to fit. By definition, marsh gas is a vaporous combustible by-product of carbohydrate and protein decomposition (*e.g.*, dead plants and animals) in swamps, bogs, and other wetlands. Chemically, it predominantly consists of methane and/or phosphine gases. Should it by some process spontaneously inflame, it would appear as small flamelike jets or bubbles of blue fire near stagnant pools. In the unlikely event that the gas would form a basketball-size shape, such dimensions would provide only enough gas volume to burn for a very brief time, and certainly not enough to allow rapid aerial maneuvers of lengthy frolics through the woods. Furthermore, it is well known among local inhabitants that there are no swamps on Brown Mountain.

Ball lightning has also been considered as a cause for the Brown Mountain Lights. While this suggestion probably has more merit than the swamp-gas theory, it's not the perfect explanation either. For example, ball lightning is a rare occurrence closely associated with thunderstorm activity. Although the Brown Mountain Lights have been reported after thunderstorms, there have also been many bona-fide sightings during fair weather. Second, this peculiar form of lightning frequently extinguishes itself with a thunderous report. Such explosive sounds are not associated with accounts of the Brown Mountain Lights.

Most popular explanations for the lights are inadequate, at best. However, about twelve years ago a viable alternative theory for some mysterious lights, including those of Brown Mountain, began to take shape.

Two scientists, Dr. Michael Persinger of Ontario, Canada, and Dr. Brian Brady of Colorado began performing research on certain luminous phenomena associated with earthquake activity. Almost simultaneously, on the cold, clear evening of November 21, 1976, William Wagner, an electronics engineer, was involved in the observation and photography of an anomaly—a basketball-size sphere of light that briefly hovered over railroad tracks in rural New Jersey. The light, which had been reported periodically for many years, was visually detected but was also photographed on infrared film and gave strong indications on electronic detection equipment. Within mere yards of the New Jersey light's century-old "haunt" lies a stem of the Long Valley earthquake fault. Interestingly, less than three weeks after the actual sighting of the light, a mild earthquake tremor was recorded in that area. Through the fieldwork of Wagner, members of New Jersey's phenomena-investigation group Vestigia, and the experimental research of Brady and Persinger, the theory of "seismic stress lights" was born.

Briefly explained, this theory prescribes that earthquake-induced pressures exerted on quartz-bearing rock in the earth's crust could possibly generate surges of extremely high voltage by a process known as the piezoelectric effect. Speculating further, these voltages could conceivably create small masses of ionized gas (plasma) near ground level. Such plasmas might take on the floating, spherical form of mysterious lights.

Presently there is no seismic data that Frizzell is aware of linking tremor activity to the appearances of the Brown Mountain Lights. However, it is interesting to note that the Grandfather Mountain fault, which is relatively old and inactive, runs very close to Brown and Chestnut mountains. While the seismic-stress theory lends itself well to an explanation for the Brown Mountain Lights, it is not yet the proved answer.

In much of the literature detailing Brown Mountain and its lights there is one persistent discrepancy that is repeatedly mentioned. Many books and periodicals have stated that "the lights are visible on almost any clear night." As a researcher who has spent many long and uneventful nights in the area, Frizzell emphatically says the statement is untrue. Appearances of the true Brown Mountain Lights, sometimes called "mineral lights" by the old-timers, are exceedingly rare events. It stands to reason that if the real phenomenon could be seen on "almost any clear night," then by now, surely, a concrete solution to the mystery would have developed.

Since that July 1978 episode, no new, significant sightings have been made. However, during the interim, the mapping of certain logging roads—which could carry four-wheel-drive vehicles and dirt bikes— has been accomplished. Mapping these crude roads was important because vehicles traveling them at night could potentially create spurious Brown Mountain Lights to observers at the Route 181 overlook.

Then there is the question of photographs. Despite literally hundreds of valid attempts, obtaining good photographs of the Brown Mountain Lights has been no easy task. Various efforts have produced black-and-white, color, and infrared prints of the phenomenon. Unfortunately, most photos are of marginal quality and therefore of little value. There are, however, some notable exceptions for all three film types. In fact, while standing on the Route 181 overlook during the mid-1960's, a Morganton man was able to take a remarkable infrared photograph of some kind of bizarre light during heavy fog conditions. Although the photograph shows a centrally lighted mass, from which spring several spiderlike radial arms, there were no visible light sources anywhere at the time he took the exposure.

Despite a few successes, generally some common problems are encountered when trying to commit the Brown Mountain Lights to film. First of all, the lights have to appear—an event which in itself is a rarity. Second, if they do appear, they are usually of short duration, giving the photographer little time to react to the situation. Third, since they do manifest themselves as point sources of light against a basically black background, three or more miles away, unless prolonged exposure times and telephoto lenses are used, resulting photographs will show only disembodied specks with virtually no frame of reference.

Getting closer to them is also a difficult task, considering that they can randomly appear just about anywhere within a nine-square-mile area of densely timbered mountainous terrain.

During joint ventures with ORION personnel, Enigma Project members made several earnest attempts to photograph the lights, within one mile of Brown Mountain, by using a fire-observation tower on Chestnut Mountain's summit. Through ORION's successful negotiations with the National Forest Service, they were permitted to use the tower for field experiments from 1979 until it was dismantled in 1981. Unfortunately, during the half-dozen or so times the towers were used, the lights never cooperated by appearing.

Continuing to investigate the seismic-stress hypothesis as a cause for the lights, ORION conceived the idea of "tickling detonations" in a modest attempt to produce the lights artificially. Again, with the generous cooperation of the Forest Service, ORION members were allowed to plant carefully controlled explosive charges on Brown and Chestnut mountains in the hope that, when detonated, they would impart sufficient seismic stress to generate a mysterious light response. In July 1981, with charges planted and cameras poised, the explosives were touched off. Subsequent photographs of the mountains during the experiments did not reveal any conclusive evidence that the Brown Mountain Lights can be produced through low-magnitude manmade stress.

In the recent past, members of ORION and the Enigma Project have used a number of experimental detection aids at the Brown Mountain site in an effort to "see" the lights beyond purely visible means. Instruments such as magnetometers (devices which detect and measure magnetic fields) have yielded little. The group has also employed infrared photography, with the same consistent lack of results. However, in order to test the seismic-stress theory adequately, some type of solid relationship must be made between any earthquake activity in the area and the appearance of the lights. Also, for the lights that do appear, spectroscopic analysis, which identifies chemical makeup of light sources, would easily eliminate such impostors as tungsten headlights, mercury-vapor lamps, and sodium-vapor lamps. In fact, during Brown Mountain excursions made in 1983 and 1984, Atlanta engineer Tom Buchanan attempted analysis of lights in the region, using a spectroscope of his own design. Although he did obtain spectral photographs of some lights, the photos were not of sufficient clarity or brightness to determine chemical composition.

Also, during the last five years, both ORION and the Enigma Project attempted the installation of seismic-telemetry equipment on Brown Mountain. This equipment would monitor, store, and transmit seismic disturbances to a receiving station fifteen miles away. These devices may have provided the connection between earthquakes and the Brown Mountain Lights—if such a connection exists. Unfortunately, these projects, plagued by technical problems and a lack of funding, have never come to full fruition.

Beyond the refraction of manmade lights and other cases of mistaken identity, no one can positively explain the mysterious balls of light that flit among the trees of Brown Mountain. Their secrets have eluded and deceived scientific inquiry for nearly a century. Outsiders are welcome to come up with answers of their own. Anyone with a car can make his or her own research trip.

The easiest way to get to Brown Mountain is by way of Morganton, a moderate-size town that lies between Hickory and Asheville along Interstate 40. Brown Mountain is located about twelve miles north of Morganton along Route 181. At about the twelve-mile point, the shoulder of Route 181 (Beatrice Cobb Highway) will open up into a large graveled parking area, which is the Route 181 Brown Mountain scenic overlook. Although there are other vantage points— such as Wiseman's View, seven miles to the west—the overlook on Route 181 is the best. From the overlook, Brown Mountain lies about 3.5 miles due east. For more adventuresome souls, it is also possible to physically ascend Brown Mountain. However, this requires careful directions from local inhabitants and the use of a four-wheel-drive vehicle.

According to the most diligent investigators, appearances of the "true" Brown Mountain Lights are waning. With each passing year, bona-fide sightings become fewer. If, in fact, legitimate appearances are declining, then there may not be enough time left to solve this mystery. The Brown Mountain Lights may die out without a resolution, and one of the earth's most interesting, enigmatic anomalies will be gone forever.

An Uninvited Visitor

This true story of possession and exorcism came to the attention of Long Island broadcasting personality Joel Martin. For the last decade, his radio and television programs have dealt with psychic and unexplained phenomena. One of his guests, whom he interviewed several times, was a gifted clairvoyant and healer named Carolina.

The details of this story were told to Joel Martin by Carolina in a private interview, which was tape-recorded. With the exception of Carolina and Joel Martin, people's names have been changed to protect the identities of those involved in a dangerous duel between good and evil. . . .

Carolina had just completed teaching her Monday-evening psychic-development class when two students asked to speak with her after the others had left. Carolina had been teaching courses in psychic development twice a week for the past six years in her home in Lindenhurst, New York, in addition to her work as a psychic-clairvoyant and healer. Her classes covered developing psychic ability, healing, mediumship, and various forms of parapsychology.

Carolina was a middle-aged woman with dark hair and eyes. The widowed mother of two sons, she had been psychic as far back as she could remember and had had her first psychic vision at the age of three.

113

She remembered playing near her father and her uncle while the men discussed the war waging in Ethiopia, which had been invaded by Mussolini's army. Suddenly Carolina felt herself leaving her body and traveling to... Ethiopia. She could clearly see Ethiopian tribesmen holding spears and coming toward her. Moments later, she began correcting her father and uncle on details of the war.

As Carolina grew, so did her powers: clairaudience (the ability to hear sounds which are not normally audible), numerology, psychometry, and healing by the laying-on of hands. When she was widowed at a young age, Carolina decided to employ her psychic abilities professionally, though she refused to accept any compensation for her healings. She considered them a gift from God to be shared.

The couple still standing in the foyer was Walter and Ruth Spencer; they were well-dressed, attractive, conservative-looking people. Both in their mid-forties, they had been attending Carolina's classes for the past month. However, this was the first time they had asked to speak with her personally.

"Do you know why we've been coming to your classes during the last four weeks?" Ruth Spencer asked nervously.

"Tell me, please," Carolina answered.

"We've been having psychic experiences in our home for the past year. We wanted to tell you about them sooner, but—" Ruth stopped in mid-sentence.

Walter Spencer continued when his wife faltered: "But to be honest, we were working up the courage to describe our problem."

"Oh, Walt, it's not really a problem," Ruth protested.

"Well, it's enough of a problem to bring us to these unusual classes to try to understand what's happening to our lives," Walter exclaimed. "I've never been open to anything concerning psychic phenomena or the supernatural!"

"Well," Carolina offered, "as long as you did come, would you like to tell me what's troubling you? Maybe I can help you with your problem."

The Spencers followed Carolina into the living room of her spacious house, perched on the edge of an overstuffed sofa, and looked uneasily at her.

"For the past year some weird things have been going on in our house," Ruth began apprehensively.

"What do you mean by 'weird'?" Carolina asked.

"We have psychic things happening in our house. For example, I see flashing lights of all different colors. It looks like sparkling lights are all around me. Orange, red, black, green. I've walked into a room to find pieces of furniture rearranged—but no one was there to do it. Sometimes the lights go on and off by themselves. On occasion I've woken up because I feel something or someone is on top of me. But there's no one. Once, something pulled me from my bed. It woke me and I screamed.

"But the worst incident—the most frightening— was a couple of months ago, when I opened my eyes to see something standing over me. It was dark in the house, but I could see it. A face, with red eyes, looked right at me. At first I thought it was human, but when I screamed in terror, it disappeared. Walter and I could find no one nor any explanation. Thinking back about it later, when I calmed down a bit, I realized it didn't look human at all.

"Walter thought I was imagining all this. And I admit I was beginning to think perhaps I *was* going crazy," Ruth explained. "But I assure you I am not inventing any of this."

"Carolina, do you have any idea what could be going on?" Walter asked.

"Are there any problems at home that you feel might be related to these occurrences?"

The Spencers glanced furtively at each other.

"To be honest, we are having problems with our daughter. Actually, it's Ruth daughter from an earlier marriage," Walter answered.

"She's a beautiful girl. Her name is Laura. She just turned eighteen," Ruth added with obvious pride.

"You let her get away with too much, Ruth. You really do spoil her," Walter protested.

Carolina interrupted. "Please don't tell me any more about your daughter or the circumstances at home. I'll try to help you. Why don't you bring Laura here and I'll do a psychic reading of her. Perhaps that way we can figure out if the disturbances in your home are somehow related to your daughter."

The following week, as Carolina had suggested, the Spencers arrived, accompanied by their daughter, Laura, who was, as her mother had said, beautiful. She had shoulder-length golden-blond hair, bright blue eyes, classical features, and porcelain skin. She looked, in fact, almost angelic.

There was something immediately peculiar, however. Laura would not look at Carolina. She kept her eyes downcast. It was as if she had agreed to come to Carolina's house, but yet chose to remain at a distance. It did not take long to comprehend this apparent contradiction: Laura was not alone. For almost immediately after meeting Laura, Carolina psychically sensed an entity with the girl. It had entered the house with her.

What Carolina saw verified what she had suspected when the Spencers first confided in her. However, she thought it wise not to say anything yet concerning her suspicions about Laura—or the entity that accompanied her.

116

Carolina decided the best course of action, for the present, was to avoid confrontation with Laura. But suddenly the girl announced that she wanted a psychic reading. Carolina sensed that this was no ordinary request—this was a challenge! Carolina accepted.

They sat face-to-face on two chairs: Carolina was purposely careful not to touch the girl. Laura still sat with her eyes downcast. Carolina did not press her. The silence wore on.

"Well, what can you tell me?" Laura finally asked in a voice that was more taunting than inquisitive.

"What do you want to know?" Carolina retorted.

"I'm searching," Laura replied abruptly.

"I know you're searching. What are you searching for?" Carolina asked.

"I'm searching for God," the girl answered, again in that mocking tone of voice.

"Why are you searching?"

Laura did not answer.

Carolina repeated her question. Again there was no response.

"Why are you searching?" Carolina persisted, however. "The kingdom of God is within you—"

Suddenly, and without warning, in response to that last remark, Laura jumped up and overturned her chair. She screamed in a hysterical frenzy. Carolina jumped to her feet in alarm over Laura's wild outburst, while Laura's parents stood stunned and helpless. Carolina's twenty-six-year-old son, Edward, a police officer, was in another part of the house. At the wild cries, he came running into the living room to witness the scene. Carolina ordered him not to interfere.

The girl was yelling and waving her arms frantically, screaming, "Get away from me! Get away from me!"

Carolina shouted back, "I'm not near you!"

117

"Get away from me! Don't touch me! Don't touch me!" Laura shrieked.

"I'm not touching you!" Carolina exclaimed. "I'm not coming near you!"

The girl looked crazed. Her face changed colors— alternating between scarlet red and ghost white. Her eyes, now crimson, were wild with rage. She threw her arms and legs in every direction, kicking over furniture and anything else that stood in her way. She screamed something unintelligible and ran from the house.

Ruth and Walter Spencer were shocked, completely devastated at the horrifying outburst, which had lasted for several minutes. When they regained their composure, their first thought was to search for their daughter. Carolina persuaded them not to. She realized what had just occurred and she knew psychically that Laura would return. While they waited, Carolina comforted the Spencers as best she could.

"What happened? I don't understand! You didn't do anything to her," Ruth cried; she was both apologetic and confused.

It was clear to Carolina that Ruth was bewildered and did not comprehend the source of Laura's outburst. Yet when she looked at Walter Spencer, she felt he suspected what was wrong with the girl. Perhaps that was because as her stepfather he could be more objective about the situation.

Although Carolina understood what had triggered the girl's tantrum, she hesitated to explain the cause aloud. Walter Spencer was skeptical and Ruth Spencer was blind where her daughter was concerned; Carolina felt they might not believe what had been apparent to her from the first moment she met the girl:

Laura Spencer was demonically possessed.

It was an evil spirit that Carolina had seen hovering around Laura and guiding her. And Carolina had immediately seen through Laura's physical beauty—to a serious psychic disturbance deep within her.

Two hours went by. Finally, as Carolina had predicted, Laura calmly walked back into the house. She showed no signs of the hysteria that had afflicted her earlier.

Ruth rushed to her daughter and hugged her. "We were so worried about you, dear," she exclaimed.

"Where were you?" Walter asked.

"I was just walking around," Laura answered coldly. She offered no other explanation.

As Carolina approached, the girl backed away. Carolina moved still closer, and Laura drew further back, sensing the psychic's intentions—to rid her of the evil spirits. Carolina had already challenged the evil in Laura. Her next course of action would have to be an exorcism—the process of purging the evil entities from the girl, through strong faith and prayers.

As Carolina went to place her hands on Laura's shoulders, the girl fought her off and moved toward the front door.

"Remember what I said," Carolina called after her. "Just remember what I said. You're searching for God, but God is within you. All the answers you're searching for are within you."

At that last remark, Laura quickly departed. Her parents meekly followed her as she bolted from the house.

Carolina knew that if she had been able to touch the girl and pray over her she would have been able to rid her of the evil entities within. However, Laura would not allow an exorcism because the evil she had permitted to enter now endowed her with a feeling of power and control—a feeling she did not want to relinquish.

Had Carolina attempted an earlier exorcism on Laura, the girl would have waged a battle so ferocious that at the time it might not have been possible to free her from the evil. Carolina would first have to physically restrain Laura, and the possessed girl was on her guard against that possibility.

Yet, Laura had come, seemingly of her own volition, to meet Carolina. Why? Carolina reasoned that while a part of Laura might have been reluctant, another part of her was deeply curious. It is a characteristic of people who are possessed that they like to taunt those who have God on their side. The evil in Laura could not resist the challenge to confront the forces of good. Demonic entities don't shrink from such defiance. In fact, the evil spirits themselves might have encouraged Laura to come face-to-face with Carolina. However, the psychic's positive words about God confronted the demons, thus setting off Laura's wild frenzy.

It was after ten P.M. and Carolina could not put out of her mind the events that had taken place earlier in the evening. She was extremely glad they were over.

She was pouring herself a cup of coffee when her thoughts were interrupted by the ringing of the telephone.

"Hello, Carolina. This is Walter Spencer. May I take a few moments of your time to talk to you in confidence about what happened earlier in your home?"

"Of course," Carolina answered.

"I think I know what's wrong with Laura—and our house," Walter said. "Do you?"

"Yes. But I didn't want to alarm you earlier or speak in front of your wife, because this is very hard to say. I've known from the first moment I met Laura that she's possessed by demonic or evil spirits. She needs help," Carolina explained.

"I was afraid you would say that. We noticed a dramatic change in Laura about a year ago. She was always quiet and introverted. As pretty as she is, she has virtually no social life or friends. But she's very intelligent.

"Her mother and I have been married for only a short time. Not quite three years. Laura was immediately resentful that her mother remarried after her divorce. Laura had been the center of attention until then, and I'm afraid I usurped her position. She probably feels she lost control of her mother.

"I fear Ruth may be on the verge of a nervous breakdown. Even so, she's very overprotective of Laura. In her eyes, Laura can do no wrong.

"Last year something changed for the worse. Laura began reading some strange books with titles that made me feel very uneasy. It was shortly after that that Ruth began complaining of those weird psychic occurrences in our house," Walter explained.

"Can you recall the books she read?" Carolina asked, knowing what the answer would be.

"Books about possession. Satanism. Devil worship. Witchcraft. Black magic. One book I found was called the *Satanic Bible*. Another was about demonology," Walter answered. "I've tried warning my wife, but she feels there's nothing to worry about. She says it's just a phase Laura's going through. What I really need to know is: what are we dealing with?" Walter asked.

"You're dealing with demons—evil forces and entities which have entered Laura and, in turn, your home. That's what possession is. It's no phase. When evil spirits possess someone, they are just using the person the way a parasite uses a host. In this case, the evil entity is the parasite and the person it has infested—Laura—is the host.

"Demonic entities use people to spread their wickedness, to capture souls in a constant struggle against God's goodness. These evil spirits come from the darkest planes of the afterlife, the netherworld, which most people call hell.

"At the same time, persons who are possessed use the evil spirits for power, greed, wickedness, wrongdoing, sin—all things that are negative. But little do they know it's not an equal exchange in the long run. People can have their lives destroyed because demons are liars. They'll say anything to get what they want. And what they want is your soul.

"The evil spirits will keep the person alive as long as they need to. Eventually they twist the person's life until the individual is destroyed psychologically and sometimes physically. Illness can result. Possession can even cause death," Carolina explained.

Walter was alarmed. "Is everyone susceptible to evil forces?" Perhaps he thought the demon entities would infect him and his wife.

"If you want power and don't care how you get it, you're susceptible," Carolina answered. "Any weakness in character or lack of faith, any severe emotional upset, when you're at your weakest—that's when evil spirits move in. It doesn't take much to allow them in. We have a choice between accepting good and accepting evil. You can say no to evil. But once you do its bidding, it can overwhelm you—you can commit terrible acts of violence."

"Recently we had an incident where Laura physically assaulted Ruth in an outburst of temper. Ruth dismissed the attack. She won't admit it, but I think she's afraid of Laura. What can be done to help Laura, to rid her of this?" Walter implored.

"The only way to free her of the demonic spirits is through exorcism. That drives them out," Carolina answered without hesitation. "Of course, demons are not so willing to let go of their victims. They'll scream horrible obscenities when they're faced with an exorcism. They can make terrible, disgusting sounds—even foul odors. They'll put up a ferocious fight; they can make objects fly around the room or break them.

Getting them out is a much harder job then letting them in. However, they do fear religious objects and prayer."

"Then the psychic disturbances in our house are definitely the result of Laura's being possessed," Walter said. "The strange lights. Objects moving. That terrible demon's face Ruth saw. The feeling of presences . . ."

Carolina confirmed his fears.

"I only hope I can convince my wife of the seriousness of the problem. We must get Laura help," Walter exclaimed.

Thoughtfully Carolina replaced the receiver on the phone. Time would tell if Walter Spencer would be successful.

The next evening, shortly before Carolina's Tuesday-night advanced psychic-development class, she received a phone call from Laura's mother, Ruth Spencer. No sooner had Carolina said hello than Ruth lashed out with an unexpected verbal barrage.

"If you read the Bible you'll see it says *you're* the product of the devil!" Ruth exhorted.

Carolina was momentarily taken aback. "I don't know what Bible you're reading, but the Bible also says there are those who are able to heal, those who are able to foresee. So we must be reading from different Bibles," she answered.

"You're the work of the devil!" Ruth repeated.

As she continued to berate Carolina, Laura's voice could be heard in the background, initiating the disconcerting accusations that Ruth obediently repeated.

Carolina made another attempt to reason with the woman. "The Bible speaks of healing and prophecies, but it warns against sorcery," she reiterated.

"I don't believe you!" Ruth exclaimed.

"Your daughter needs help," Carolina said.

"I should have listened to my daughter and never gone to see you," Ruth answered.

"I can't force you to come back to me if you don't want to. You have to do what's best for you. God be with you. You're going to need him!" Carolina replied.

It was pointless to argue. Carolina knew that she could no longer hope to administer an exorcism to Laura. Her involvement with this dangerous girl seemed to be over. And she had little time to dwell on the problems of the Spencers: her students were arriving.

She began the psychic-development class by saying, "You know, we had a very strange experience here last night..."

She thought the incident was a good example of a true, although disturbing, episode of demonic possession that students of psychic phenomena might learn from. Carolina began describing what had happened the previous evening—how Laura had bolted from her, screaming hysterically, running from the house. As she spoke, she noticed that her son Edward had arrived home from work. He walked quietly to his room. A moment later she was abruptly interrupted by his voice calling for her.

"Ma, please get in here now!" he shouted.

"What's the matter?" she asked, surprised by the unusual interruption.

"Please get in here!" he again demanded.

Carolina immediately left the class and ran to her son's room. She stopped in the doorway and saw that he was staring helplessly at one corner of the room. For years, a cross had hung on the wall there, and several religious statues sat neatly on a large dresser. However, that was not the case now.

The cross had been ripped from the wall and thrown to the floor, facedown. The religious statues had all mysteriously been turned around so that they were now backward—facing the wall.

Carolina hurried to the other rooms of the house. Edward followed. She went first to what had been her late mother's room. Here, too, religious figures had all been turned around to face the walls. A cross had been knocked down and thrown to the floor. At this point a confused Edward left and walked back to his room.

Carolina quickly went next to her own bedroom. The scene here was identical. Statues of Jesus, St. Anthony, and the Virgin Mary had all been reversed in the same manner. As in the other rooms, a cross over her bed had been torn from the wall and flung to the floor. This crucifix, too, was now facedown. A painting of Jesus Christ was similarly inverted.

Carolina suddenly realized that the part of the house where all the bedrooms were felt ice cold. It was as if all at once she had walked into a refrigerator. Yet the living room, where the class remained, was not cold at all. That part of the house remained warm. Only in the rooms where there were overturned religious objects was it abnormally cold.

Carolina had been careful not to touch anything. She just stood and stared numbly at the sight of Roman Catholic religious articles and figures facing backward and downward. Unexpectedly, the quiet was broken by another scream from Edward.

"Ma, come in here!" he yelled.

She ran to him and was greeted by the sight of a terror-stricken Edward standing straight as a rail.

"Look at this! I didn't touch it, I didn't put it or this way! I swear to God I didn't," he exclaimed. Edward pointed to the gold cross he wore on a chain around his neck. The crucifix was completely turned around, as if it had been placed that way on the chain. Except that it had not been done by Edward. The figure of Jesus Christ on the cross, which should have faced outward, instead was facing inward, toward his chest.

Carolina looked at Edward. He was not ordinarily the fearful type. Yet he stood petrified before her, unwilling to touch the crucifix. Now she finally understood the fiendish occurrences transpiring in her home. They were the work of demonic spirits—diabolical entities commanded by Laura Spencer!

"I didn't do this!" Edward exclaimed. "I swear it!"

"I know you didn't. Stay calm. Don't touch it," Carolina reassured him. "Listen to me. The very fear of evil makes the evil spirits that did this grow in strength. They like to play psychological games. Turning religious objects and pictures upside down is meaningless. It's meant to scare and weaken us, to make us susceptible to possession. But demons can't take God from our souls this way—unless we let them. Understand that God is stronger than the devil. Nothing can overcome God!"

With those words from his mother, Edward began to calm down noticeably.

Curious students from Carolina's class watched in stunned silence. She provided them with a cursory explanation of the events, and then dismissed them until next week's class.

Carolina knew exactly what she had to do next. Exorcisms would have to be performed on Edward and the rooms where the religious articles had been disturbed. In fact, everything in the house—the entire house—would have to be exorcised, purged of the demonic entities which, even now, might be poised to strike again at any moment. Carolina realized that when Laura had run from the house the day before, she had not been walking in the neighborhood as she claimed. Rather, the girl had circled the house, summoning, through demonic chants, entities to help her—evil entities that she had left in Carolina's home to prove that she was in control. The evil spirits had obeyed Laura's command by upsetting the religious objects they hated and feared so intently. When Carolina had spoken to her class about Laura, it was the trigger for the demonic spirits to unleash their fury.

For the girl to have caused this, she had to be possessed of a great amount of demonic power. Not enough, however, for a confrontation with Carolina or to withstand an exorcism. For if that had been the case, Laura would not have fled the house. She knew the forces of God were more powerful than Satan.

Now Carolina proceeded to apply, to her son and home, the powerful prayers of the ancient rites of exorcism as it has been practiced in the Roman Catholic Church for centuries.

First she made the sign of the cross and said a special prayer to protect herself. Then she sprinkled Holy Water on the affected areas and read aloud: "I exorcise and command thee, O Spirit . . . I cast thee out. . . ."

She walked throughout the house, Edward following in her footsteps, invoking the positive energy of prayer and her strong faith in God. She summoned his soldiers: "St. Michael, pray for us. St. Gabriel, pray for us. All the sacred angels and archangels, pray for us, pray for us. . . ."

She moved from room to room, commanding the spirits to leave, repeatedly invoking prayers and thus putting protection around the house. The process continued for some twenty minutes. Finally she sensed the demons withdrawing. The bedrooms were once again warming to their normal temperature.

Next she went to every room, carefully turning each religious statue frontward, in the original direction it had faced, prior to the misdeeds of the evil spirits. She placed the painting of Jesus Christ back in its proper position; she rehung the crucifixes so they all faced outward. Before each article, she paused and waited, and watched in relief. Every religious article remained exactly as she placed it.

Now Edward carefully removed the cross from around his neck and switched the direction it faced. It was, once again, correctly facing outward. Carolina was certain the harrowing ordeal was now over. She had forced the spirits of darkness back to Laura Spencer, from whom they had originated.

But if the danger had passed for Carolina, it was, tragically, to continue for Laura and her parents. Carolina knew what the future held for them. Through her own choice, Laura would remain possessed—and she would next turn the full fury of her demonic powers on a new victim.

Laura's mother was an emotionally weak woman, easily manipulated by her daughter and therefore susceptible to the danger of possession. Laura's deepseated resentment would manifest itself in only one way. The girl would unleash her demonic powers on her own mother, who was not strong enough to withstand the invasion by evil spirits. And Walter Spencer's only chance for survival would be to leave his wife and stepdaughter, who were condemned—in this life and the next—to do the devil's work.

Carolina knew there were many others like Laura: anonymous, faceless people in the cities and the suburbs, moving among us today . . . and demonically possessed. There was no way to know when she'd next meet one of them, when another "Laura" might come into her life.

Perhaps that explains why Carolina walks through her house each morning, checking her many religious statues and articles, to be certain they are all facing in exactly the right direction. . . .

Where Time Stands Still

Mystery Hill is a megalithic structure in New Hampshire that is thought to be over four thousand years old. Its purpose and its builders are unknown. But two things are known about it. The first is that its builders believed in blood sacrifice. The second is that many of the structures mark important astrological events—hence its other name: America's Stonehenge.

Jim Knusch is the media representative for Mystery Hill. His records contain incredible stories that the average tourist will never hear, and he has graciously made this information available to readers of True Tales.

In the wide search for answers to the question "What is Mystery Hill?" the search has gone beyond the realms of archaeology and science. What you are about to read is the history of the psychic exploration of "America's Stonehenge."

The sun rises in North Salem, New Hampshire, casting precisely calculated shadows over standing stones which have been carbon-dated at more than four thousand years old. This is America's Stonehenge, one of the largest and possibly oldest megalithic sites in North America.

Once called Cowbell Corners and Pattee's Caves (although these are not truly caves), the area is now named Mystery Hill. The 110-square-acre site was opened to the public twenty years ago by the privately owned Mystery Hill Corporation, headed by Robert E. Stone. It has a state historical status because of its connection with the Underground Railway during the Civil War, as well as its importance during colonial times.

Although the stone structures cover twenty of the 110 acres, less than one acre is actually excavated. But what can be found on that one acre has attracted not only archaeologists but also physicists and psychics.

Visitors to the site are given a pamphlet that lists and explains all the points of interest. After leaving the cabin/museum, one walks up a trail, past erratic double stone walls that enclose the site, and encounters the first feature, the Watchhouse, whose purpose is yet unknown. The structure has been of great interest to researchers because it is the only chamber not contained within the main site and it is thought to be an outpost or guardhouse.

From the Watchhouse a double-walled processional path leads to the main complex. There are quite a number of stone chambers and structures, standing stones, and walled areas. Nearby, in the swamp area, is a gigantic clay deposit, which may explain why an ancient culture would settle there. A large fire pit to the west may also have been used in making pottery.

An excavated well, called the Well of the Crystals, contains quartz crystals in a natural vertical fault located twenty-two feet down. Crystals were worshiped or used for tools by many ancient cultures. There are also a crudely carved sundial and astronomically aligned walls and platforms.

The stone is indigenous to the surrounding area, and the standing stones are hand-worked and generally triangular-shaped. Most of the "buildings" are about five feet high and contain chambers. The roofs of these structures are capstones weighing between six and ten tons.

The Oracle Chamber is the one fully intact structure and it is also the most important. Inside this chamber, which visitors can walk through, is a hieroglyph of a running deer or ibex, fireplace openings, a closet, niches, and a "speaking tube." It has been theorized that this speaking tube was used by priests, hidden inside the chamber, who pretended their disembodied voices belonged to the gods. Outside the Oracle Chamber is a four-and-one-half-ton grooved slab of stone supported by stone legs. The speaking tube leads from the Oracle Chamber to directly under the giant slab, which is known as the Sacrificial Table. The groove in the table runs parallel to the outside perimeter, and is reminiscent of the groove in a meat platter. Indeed, underneath the inner structure is a network of drains that are still functional. The slab was probably used in blood sacrifices, according to scientists, researchers, psychics and other professionals who have investigated the site.

The outside area contains monoliths which are arranged in a definite circular pattern around the outer perimeter of the main site. The shaped standing stones are in exact locations that mark important astronomical events, such as the annual summer and winter solstices (June 21 and December 21) and the equinoxes (March 22 and September 22). It also marks a number of minor ones, such as the sunrises and sunsets on May 1, August 1, February 1, and November 1. Many of the dates coincide with ancient pre-Christian holidays. From a central point—the Sacrificial Table—the sun will rise and set over the appropriate monoliths. Hence the name America's Stonehenge.

Who were the original builders of America's Stonehenge at Mystery Hill? The Amerindians? European travelers? A totally unknown and different native culture? Extraterrestrials? None of the above? Scientists and psychics have tried to find the answers, but in totally different ways.

Mystery Hill is estimated to be four thousand years old. Not much is known about this period of time in America. We do know what was happening in other parts of the world. In Europe the Early Bronze Age was about 2500 B.C. Between 2000 and 1500 B.C., during the second-millennium Bronze Age, the Minoans, whose civilization historians consider one of the most brilliant in antiquity, were formalizing the first true writing (as opposed to pictographs and hieroglyphics). In ancient Egypt, the Middle Kingdom thrived between 1900 and 1800 B.C. Moses led the Israelites out of Egypt in 1250 B.C. In ancient China the first dynasty was founded somewhere between 2205 and 1557 B.C. In the Yucatán, the Mayans' formative period was from 1200 B.C. to A.D. 300, while other cultures like the Zapotec and the Olmec were just beginning. Aeons before the Incas in the Peruvian Andes, the oldest known culture of that era was the Chavin, who began between 1200 and 800 B.C. and lasted until about 400 B.C. And what is known of the small nomadic bands of Amerindians of early New Hampshire is that they were dwelling either in caves or in wooden huts. Arguments over whether or not Mystery Hill was built by natives, Europeans, seafaring cultures, or South and Central American Indians still continue.

David Stewart-Smith is a master mason and director of restoration at Mystery Hill. He feels that the nearby stone quarries (not included in the visitors' pamphlet) are "the one spot where we come closest to the original builders of America's Stonehenge." The quarried material reveals stone worked by stone, point-ing to a pre-Iron Age people. Stewart-Smith has also uncovered a point on the grounds which he has deter-mined as possibly the earliest part of the site, built several years earlier and away from the main body of structures. It is here (referred to as Mystery Hill 1), according to Stewart-Smith, that one supervising the setting-up of the outer walls and first astronomical alignments could call to the laborers and direct the marking stones to be moved into proper positions. It is his theory that the calendar was set up first and the "temple" later built within its interior.

Yet Stewart-Smith's associate and senior staff researcher, W. E. S. Hinton Jr., disagrees on certain elements involving the order in which Mystery Hill was constructed. It is his theory that the site was first a gathering place, then a hill fort, long before it was considered a good point for astronomical observation. Hinton states that "whoever built Mystery Hill used only stone tools, and used a technique that is not used structurally anywhere in the world but the greater New England area. To be from Europe, these people would have had to be here for a long time, out of contact—no mass trade, no communication whatsoever—to have lost their culture and their technology." Hinton also thought that the builders of Mystery Hill were the proto-Hopewell-Adena culture—proved to have been the Midwest mound builders. Agreeing with Hinton's theo-ries is the noted archaeo-astronomical researcher Byron Dix, who felt that there were similarities between the temple-mound "cities" of the Midwest and the Vermont calendar sites that he brought to light. At a symposium in the spring of 1984, Dix attributed all the sites to the Hopewellian cultures.

All three men agree totally on another theory regarding the original builders of America's Stone-henge: they do not appear to have been of European origin, but rather a culture indigenous to this continent—perhaps an unknown culture of Amerindians.

This, however, is totally contrary to Robert Stone's research, which clearly shows European influences. Established facts and observations of similarities with ancient European sites are numerous. Megalithic structures, dating back in antiquity and scattered throughout England, Ireland, France, Scotland, Spain, and Portugal, resemble a master building plan in stone that could have made the voyage with their architects across thousands of miles of ocean. On the Iberian Peninsula, at a latitude of 42, 52.8°, is Cape Finisterre, a small fishing port with ancient Celtic megalithic ruins. It is commonly believed that no astronomical calendars exist there, but there are stone structures that bear a striking resemblance to the structures in southern New Hampshire. What could be so unique about this particular European site? The latitude of America's Stonehenge is 42, 50.4°. These ancient travelers, if they were truly connected with what is now North Salem, certainly knew their geometry. Any latitude within an orb of forty-five degrees will be excellent for equinoctal measurements.

Perhaps they desired to build a house for their deity and devoted much time to the task. It has been suggested that Mystery Hill is a temple to a sun god and just happened to be constructed along with an astronomical calendar. But assuming the existence of divine revelation and a gifted person's ability to "sense" where the best geographical location would be to practice religious rites, one could accept the fact that a high priest might have determined that on Mystery Hill the energies and holy elements would be the strongest.

Curiously, some hewn stones were found midway between the quarry and the main site, indicating that at one point the builders ceased their activities and could have left their work unfinished. Why did they stop? Where did they go? How much was left to build?

America's Stonehenge has at various times been visited and written about by accomplished writers and researchers. The distinguished epigrapher and leading authority on ancient languages Dr. Barry Fell devotes much literary space to the site in one of his books, *America, B.C.* Charles Michael Boland's *They All Discovered America* devoted a chapter to Pattee's Caves. In her research for her novel *Avalon*, published in 1965, Anya Seton pays a debt to the "extraordinary 'Place of Stones' on the Merrimack, at North Salem aptly called 'Mystery Hill'." None of these writers, however, have commented on the astronomical alignments. This oversight can be simply explained. No astronomical alignments were ever considered at the site until Robert Stone read Gerald Hawkins' book *Stonehenge Decoded* (1965). Since the astronomical alignments were "rediscovered" on the Salisbury Plain, could the same happen in southern New Hampshire? Following that reading and more research, broad swaths were cut through the hundreds of trees in the surrounding woods beyond the outer walls of the site. This was done in order to observe certain standing stones clearly from the main part of the site.

This work paid off, for on December 21, 1970, Stone succeeded in photographing a series of pictures that indeed showed the sun setting over one of these monoliths. For the first time in possibly thousands of years, a living being actively observed the winter-solstice sunset from within the confines of this unique tract of land. This series of slides taken at two-minute intervals is still one of the best-selling items in the site's gift shop. The interested public can observe the alignments during the spring, summer, and fall and by special arrangement during the winter.

Perhaps the most controversial element of America's Stonehenge's many puzzles, and another tie to European influence, is the Sacrificial Table (also referred to as the "grooved slab"). On this table both animal and human sacrifice was practiced. Since the person or animal sacrificed would be elevated to the holiest of levels (as was the case in numerous ancient cultures, including the Mayans and several pre-Iron Age sects), the blood would be collected and revered. One can easily accept the fact that the stone's groove, with the needed runoff cut, would be utilized in the ceremony. In his 1961 book, *They All Discovered America*, author Charles Michael Boland cites this very reason—blood sacrifice—as *the* primary motivating force in the migration of ancient travelers to these shores and what is now southern New Hampshire. A relatively small sect of practitioners were forced from their homes, quite possibly in Europe, and boldly ventured to a land far across the sea (to a place that they might have heard about from other travelers?) and settled where they would be free from persecution and free to continue their activities. One can also imagine generations continuing, forgetting their European roots—but only to a point—and even teaching their ways to the natives, who would pick up the rites and practices, adding to and subtracting from them as the centuries passed by. The dedicated researcher must take into account such possible events and place them in their proper perspective. Where visible evidence is lacking, the psychic and the sensitive can aid in the quest.

Psychic exploration of America's Stonehenge has had a spotted and erratic history. Brought there by others or visiting the grounds on their own, psychics usually gather impressions while walking among and physically touching what can be found there. Others, who have never set foot on the site, have performed psychometries (the process of divining knowledge about an object or a person connected with it through contact with the object) on small stones, crystals, and various other objects borrowed from the site. Still others have simply "tuned in" during séance trance states. In charting the transcriptions of these diverse readings, both close similarities and vast differences have come to light. All investigators, however, agree on certain elements: the site's origins date back thousands of years; strong energies inherent in the locale and/or from the powers of the earliest occupants definitely exist; and most of the physical evidence that archaeological digs are searching for is irretrievably lost.

The earliest long-distance psychometry on record occurred in Ojai, California. It was performed by Margarette Winspear (not her real name) in March 1967. How this came about is interesting. Jim Black (not his real name), the manager of the site at that time, was a ham radio enthusiast, and he first met the Winspears years ago over the radio—when he lived in Florida and they were visiting in Costa Rica! They were friends for a long time before Jim asked her to try her psychic abilities on the site. Although she considered herself essentially a healer, as a personal favor to Black, Margarette reluctantly psychometrized a quartz crystal taken from the site. She was amazed when the reading went on for two and a half hours!

In the beginning, Margarette first *became* the crystal and vaguely described the areas of the site. Slabs of stone were seen as reddish-brown colored. A "sacrificial table" of some sort was mentioned, as was the practice of blood sacrifice—animal, not human. She felt that the activities were evil because of the ceremonies occurring in secret. Still being the crystal, she then saw that its origin was not on this continent at all, but rather in northern England, first touched by human hands around "the time of the Celts," not pinpointing a specific time. The journey of the crystal from the old world to the new occurred a few years after the discovery of America (again not a specific time, presumably after Columbus' first voyage), after being handed down through many generations.

The time then became much, much earlier, possibly by thousands of years. The earliest tribes of Amerindians

137

are observed avoiding the area and are asked why they do so. Their response: because of the secret ceremonies going on there. Ancient inhabitants come into view: twelve men dressed like monks. These twelve "monks" are ruling a small group of men who are laboring, constructing the site. A general overview of the original plan of the site is not seen. The twelve, however, are described by Margarette Winspear as tall, pale luminescent skin, dark-eyed, totally hairless, flat noses, round cheekbones, not resembling any particular race identifiable on earth, yet definitely native to this planet. The other men, about twenty-five or thirty in all, are described as dark-skinned, with black hair, almost Amerindian, wearing similar robes. The surrounding terrain is barren—rightly so, because four thousand years ago the area would have been predominantly bedrock. These twelve leaders and their followers are observed chanting, controlling natural elements like lightning, and ritualistically performing sacrifices by fire. Their clothing seems made of unidentifiable material, possibly synthetic, and as they move, they seem to defy gravity.

Margarette then managed to view the key activities of the entire globe. In these days of antiquity, concurrent with what was happening in what is today southern New Hampshire, she sees no white men in either North or South America, and great civilizations in Asia, India, China, and Egypt, which are in communication with each other. The continents are now seen all connected in one way or another, with less water in the oceans and many more islands. Europe is populated by barbarians, while ancient Amerindian tribes are flourishing in the Americas. The time was prime for global travel, and enough of an exchange of cultures occurred to account for similarities in these faraway places. This unique small band of twelve men, however, is the last of a superior race numbering about five hundred that originated in the area of the site (or evolved from an even earlier, ancient race) and soon died out. Almost immediately after that, *all* the occupants perish in a massive landslide, which doesn't cover the main site. The area stays unoccupied and is avoided by the growing tribes of the Amerindians for the next (undisclosed) thousands of years. Margarette's conclusion was that this fine, elite race died out because of some sort of cataclysm brought about by the aforementioned evil nature of their practices.

The next psychic exploration involved Marc Donald (not his real name), a fellow engineer who worked with Robert Stone at Western Electric in 1973. Marc Donald had never set foot on Mystery Hill. Yet, seated behind his desk at work, Donald was able to give close descriptions of America's Stonehenge.

Being interested in archaeology and ancient civilizations, he felt strong impressions about the site and about Sprite Pond in Maine, another site Stone was involved with at the time. Never having seen them, Donald was able to describe the shapes, sizes, and arrangements of the structures. Donald made a point of explaining that he accomplished his reading by going into an "alpha state" and firmly held no belief in any sort of "spirit guide."

The next psychic probe took place in 1974, using a map of America's Stonehenge and a telephone. Ernest Goodryder, of the Institute of Psychic Insight of Elizabeth, New Jersey, also was a former member of the New England Antiquities and Research Association and made the acquaintance of Bob Stone through that organization. His purpose was to explore, through several psychics of his own choice, early establishments throughout New England. During the sessions, the bulk of the questioning centered on the site at Mystery Hill. The era in question reached back thousands of years—before, Goodryder believed, there had been a polar shift.

The modus operandi was to send a map to the psychic, then contact the psychic by phone and record the sessions. Of the many psychics recruited for this ongoing project, two of note were Reverend Josephine Shafer and Reverend Verna Wilson. The questions asked were basically the same in each case. The official title of Goodryder's project was "The Prehistoric Astrology Civilizations of the North Atlantic." As far as is known, none of the psychics were in contact with each other or had visited the site previously.

Josephine Shafer at first saw the earliest inhabitants to be dark-skinned, possibly American Indians or blacks, wearing very little. She also saw what appeared to be monks and nuns. The climate of this era, thousands of years ago, was more temperate. Goodryder, as previously mentioned, attributed this to the shift of the poles—the ancient south and north poles having exchanged positions. These ancient people spoke a unique and now-long-lost language. Blood sacrifice was definitely practiced, possibly human, but she did not see any specific methods used. Communication with other civilizations around the world was occurring. They were also in touch with Atlantis and were ahead of the Atlanteans spiritually. A mention was also made of the fact that the red men, the American Indians, were the descendants of the Atlanteans and not the builders of America's Stonehenge. She saw them observing the rites and ceremonies with interest but from a distance. Their behavior heralds that of the Amerindians, who avoided the site in later eras.

It was strongly felt that these ancient people were *not* native to what is now North America. Wherever they migrated from, they did so of their own free will. Boland, in *They All Discovered America*, makes a point of positing that *the* reason for emigrating was to escape religious persecution stemming from their driving need to practice ritualistic blood sacrifice. The only other reason that ancient societies would travel to unknown and possibly extremely dangerous regions was in quest of high adventure and profit, especially at a time when such global exploration required uncommon skills and years of travel time. The Vikings, for example, conceivably would not take the time to build stone temples, set up astronomical calendars, and remain to celebrate religious days throughout the year.

Although Reverend Shafer established that these earliest inhabitants were not from Atlantis, she saw them migrating from a place on earth that had sunk beneath the ocean. The only hint as to the possible name of their place of origin, or any other particular place, was a word that she couldn't pronounce that started with the letter M. (She had no thought when asked if these ancient builders were also the builders of Stonehenge.) They looked upon the female as inferior. Fire became a prominent element, possibly used not only for heat and light but also for close-proximity communication. Some cattle were present, as was farming—hence one of the needs for astronomical information.

Colonies as far south as Cape Cod and as far north as Canada were evident, and Goodryder made note of a possible "Junior Stonehenge" in Bucksport, Maine. Reverend Shafer added that she felt the aftermath of some sort of cataclysm. She also drew a correlation between the New Hampshire site and other ancient structures in places like Sweden and France.

Now, attempting to tune in on energies of the site itself, questions and answers went as follows:

Q: How much of Mystery Hill is visible?

Shafer: The majority is covered up.

Q: How far down will Bob Stone have to dig to make any significant finds?

Shafer: Oh, maybe as far down as ten feet.

Q: What do you think he'll find?

Shafer: I believe, some sort of plates, maybe stone tablets of some sort. These written chiseled documents may have a message for mankind.

Q: Where should he search for any evidence of these ancient people?

Shafer: Further outside the main site, where living establishments were.

(Since she gave no specific direction as to where Bob Stone should dig, the remaining 109 acres would be a long and involved project indeed.)

Q: Finally, why did they choose there, in what is now North Salem?

Shafer: I feel these people could mentally communicate with each other as well as tune in to strong energies and natural elements. The stones themselves are charged powerfully with these energies, energies other than magnetism, of natural origin.

Ernest Goodryder's interview with Reverend Verna Wilson yielded many similarities, with a few slight variations. She immediately envisioned the site and actually described some of the major features. Again, the era being explored was thousands of years back. Again, there were dark-skinned people, Atlantean connections, and a cataclysm. As far as sacrifices, gruesome ones were evident, but descriptions of the methods used weren't mentioned. A plate, possibly with an important message inscribed on it, was seen "on a slope." When asked if she could put a name to the site or to its early inhabitants, she couldn't think of any one particular word.

Reverend Wilson felt that America's Stonehenge was part of a large colony, not only in New England but also throughout North America. Small groups were spread out over large distances. They were all in communication with each other, as well as with civilizations in diverse parts of the world. At times they communicated psychically. She strongly felt that they were highly advanced, yet was not specific as to whether they were advanced just for their own time or by our own present standards. A carving in the shape of the letter T, which Reverend Wilson felt had some sort of Egyptian connection, was mentioned. Its location was not revealed. However, the strongest similarity to Reverend Shafer's insights were Reverend Wilson's feelings of these ancient people's strong psychic powers: not only were they dependent upon the sun as a means for charting the seasons and establishing holy days, but they had a strong psychic link to the sun and may have almost had the ability to draw down this energy from the sun.

In 1983, a psychometry involving a small collection of stones, a mini-cairn if you will, was performed in a commercial radio station. It was simultaneously recorded on audiotape for a future broadcast and on videotape for inclusion in a documentary. Jim Knusch, the media representative of America's Stonehenge, had regularly appeared on Joel Martin's radio talk show as well as the cable TV show *Psychic Channels*, hosted by Joel Martin and the nationally known psychic medium George Anderson. Anderson has aided law-enforcement agencies in locating missing persons, and has been written about in several periodicals.

During one particular *Psychic Channels* episode, the question of previous psychic exploration of Mystery Hill was discussed and Joel and Jim, on the air, asked George if he would be willing to try. Although he prefers to keep a low profile, and was extremely busy with private readings, George said, "Sure, I'll give it a shot." The stage was set to add one more chapter to the psychic exploration of America's Stonehenge.

On a rainy late-summer afternoon in Babylon, Long Island's WBAB radio station, George was busy with a full schedule. His first task was to attempt to contact the departed spirit of a child recently murdered by three teenagers, and then the cameras would be set up to record his impressions of Mystery Hill. Joel Martin assured his radio listeners that this night's program would be very different. And, in fact, the psychometry experiment lasted approximately forty minutes and the radio show had to be extended to an hour. A previous incident involving George's first physical contact with the energies locked within the small pile of stones was also discussed during the recording session.

TRANSCRIPTION OF THE WBAB RADIO PSYCHOMETRY PERFORMED BY PSYCHIC GEORGE ANDERSON ON APRIL 26, 1983:

Joel Martin: This is going to be a very unusual radio program. Psychic medium George Anderson is by my side—not for call-ins. This is an experiment. Jim Knusch is on the other side of the table: researcher, television producer working on a documentary called *Enigma of the Ancients*. And we'll be talking about a place we will introduce to you soon as the Stonehenge of North America. At the very same time we are talking, we are being videotaped. But I thought I'd explain that if you hear some unusual noises, it's not spirits rattling around, but videotape equipment, some people, and some lights—very unusual for a radio program.

[After a few introductory comments involving the site, its name and location, description, and theories—and of course comparisons with Stonehenge in England—we get around to the psychometry. Several stones are taken out of a plain brown bag and placed on the table in front of George. While this is being done, Joel relates a story about what happened when he gave these very same stones to George a few months ago.]

Joel: Can I tell you of that very briefly? I think that it's very important. A few months ago Jim gave me a paper bag filled with stones, large, very attractive rocks. They looked like rocks from anyone's garden. I brought them down to the TV studio one night when George and I were taping a cable show. I had him look at these stones and, I swear, I told him nothing. All I said was that I got some stones here from a friend's garden. I took them out of the large paper bag and in a second he put his hands over his face [he gestures the same] and said, "Gaaah! These are covered with blood!" I said, "What?" George said, "They must have been used for some sort of human sacrifice." Jim later confirmed that one part of the site may indeed have been used for blood sacrifice.

[Jim speaks to George for a few minutes. The repulsion that George felt about the blood on the rocks should not happen again, now that he is "familiar" with them. He is to concentrate on the *who* and *when* regarding the original designers and/or builders of the site. He is also asked to relate any words or names that might come to him. Hopefully, images of the locale or physical attributes of the long-bygone residents may manifest.]

George (joking): Let's take a moment here to warm up on the "time tunnel."

Joel: Let me describe what is going on. Jim Knusch has just taken out of a large paper bag several of the stones that are being given to George. The video camera is, of course, recording that. Let me describe that George is holding them now, and that is called psychometrizing— being able to determine something of the being or the history of the artifacts from just holding and sensing and feeling psychically. George is studying them right now. He is holding two of the smaller ones. There is a total of, ah, seven.

George: The first impression that I receive is: there seems to have been a cataclysm prior to the building of this community, civilization, whatever you want to call it. It almost looks like some sort of atomic blast. I *am* seeing an atomic blast. I'm going back definitely before the time of the Christ. It's funny, I see a marvelous civilization prior to this one. I see an atomic blast, people in fear and darkness. The people in this Stonehenge give me the

145

impression that they're survivors of this atomic blast, of
this civilization, or descendants of these people. And if
I'm not mistaken, a lot of these structures were built
half under the ground?

Joel: Can you acknowledge that, Jim?

George: Because it's for purifying purposes like
from radiation or something, like there's been a poison
released from this cataclysm.

Jim: Several structures are at present half under
the ground. But that's mainly because in the past few
thousand years topsoil has blown up around the structures, burying them. The bulk of the structures were
hewn into the bedrock and the inhabitants stood above
and below these dolmens and stone huts.

George, do any words come to mind? Descriptions
of any persons, possibly names?

George: To be honest with you, I'm hearing a
language that I've never heard before in my life. I can't
hear it clear enough to make out a word as of yet. There
seems to be a lot of chanting.

Jim: Possibly names? If it sounds like gibberish,
just say it, blurt it out.

George: I keep getting N-i-j-a-n. I don't know if it's
a person or a place. I'm just going to give out everything that I see. I don't understand a word of it, but I'll
do it anyway. There is also [pause], the people seem to
be, it's almost as if they've been set back out of fear. It's
odd, I want to say that their community or civilization is
barbaric, but it's not. The people seem to be bronze-
skinned or red-skinned, although they do not look like
American Indians. I keep seeing, I keep hearing chanting, and it sounds like a community of monks, not
associated with Catholicism, and they are all wearing
hoods of some sort. They almost look like the Ku Klux
Klan. Was it true that someone lived under the sacrificial slab?

Jim: Well, there is an underground cavern, man-made, adjacent to the slab.

George: They're going underground. They're going under it. Is there any evidence that these people were warlike at any time?

Jim: That's part of the enigma. If they were warlike, that's what I want to know.

George: I'm getting the impression that there is the deep fear of war. Would the human hand be used a great deal in the symbology on the carvings or anything? Or anything symbolizing the hand? I'm getting pain in the right hand, as if it's been overworked.

Jim: What we do know is that they did do a lot of working, as most people do with their hands, possibly involving the stonemasonry with constructing the site.

George: But there also seems to be a lot of symbolism connected with it. Definitely, the community seems to be living in fear, not of each other but of outsiders. It's a very autonomous community. [Pause.] It's also interesting, I don't see any children. I see young adults, up to middle age and older.

Jim: Can you describe what they're wearing? Do you see how they look?

George: It seems like tunics of some sort. And I keep hearing this word "Nijan" or something like that. It's almost as if this word stands for a singular purpose. There seems to be some sort of decoration around the eyes of the men wearing robes. There's some sort of spiritual purpose. It's almost like Europe being put back into the Dark Ages. The civilization seems to have been advanced, but because of this cataclysm, fear has set them back. Did they have any kind of underground drainage or water or something like that?

Jim: There is a complex drainage system running under the main part of the site. Do you see it as part of the original construction? That's what I want to know.

George: I see it as a carry-over from this earlier civilization.

Jim: Do you get an impression of the design, shape, of the original constructions? Possibly the builders? Original occupants?

George: It seems that these people have fled from another continent or another area, not far from where they were. I've got to be honest with you, I feel some strong Atlantean connections. They were aware of the cataclysm that was about to take place and managed to get away, or experienced the cataclysm, survived it, took refuge in this part of what is now the United States. The older people, especially the men, seem to be the wiser ones. They have the knowledge of this drainage system. They have the scientific mind, I'd like to say, to build these homes semiunderground, I guess, to prevent radiation or whatever poison contact came out of that. They also conduct the spiritual ceremonies. They seem to be vegetarians. I see nothing but plants around. Sheep are around, though; they seem to be sacred, or have a sacred use—perhaps sacrificial—they have a saintly role in the civilization. It seems to be a very socialistic community too. Everyone has a specific role. Their dress seems to give me what position they play in this community. The priests would wear the robes, craftsmen would wear the tunic.

It sounds as if someone is saying the word "Helen" or "Helena." I don't know whether it's a name or just another word. And a staff seems to have a particular purpose. The older ones carry staffs. Also, because of this cataclysm, there's been a complete loss of time. The reason why the buildings and structures are set accordingly is that they're able to tell the season or the time because of the sun's rotation accordingly: there's a particular structure the sun is appearing on and it's cold out, they know just what part of the winter they're in. It seems that their system of astronomy or time has

148

been disrupted, but they're aware of it. Because of the cataclysm. The older crowd is aware of it, putting it into focus.

[Joel at this point reidentifies the radio station, show, and what has been going on. George then comments on the impressions of the individual stones. One in particular he feels has come from some sort of ruling structure. Jim then informs him that the stones were taken from diverse places around the site, even from down near the entrance to the site, from the main road.]

George: It seems as if these people were wearing some sort of a mask on their faces, almost like a gas mask. There's something being worn on the face when they're out of the home. Strange, you could almost take them as being from another planet, although there's definitely no connection with anything extraterrestrial.

Jim: One last request for any words that may exist. Again, no matter if they sound like gibberish, say them anyway.

George: The language seems to have a double sound. Like the K sound in our language. I see in their language a capital K next to a lower-case K. It would be emphasized on the sound in a double sense. As if I would say, "Ki-Kk-Kik." Like that. And this would go down the entire alphabet.

Jim: Possibly any phrases or chants?

George: No, it's funny, every time you mention that, I see the word N-i-j-a-n. It's a large capital N and then they now change it to a small N. The way all the words are pronounced, the sounds all have a meaning. They all seem to be, shall I say, "in tune" with nature. Everything seems to be in a proper balance because they feel that this cataclysm that caused the destruction of this civilization threw their, ah, because of their imbalance of nature, this was the cause of it. It definitely seems to be a community that lives by the book, out of fear of something that's happened. I keep getting that emphasis on it. It doesn't seem to be a civilization that was used to any hard or physical work prior to this.

[George then asks about any known "lines of communication" that may have been used by the ancients at America's Stonehenge, because of his constantly seeing what look like telephone poles. He then interprets this as a symbol of their being able to communicate, almost on a one-to-one basis, telepathically. The sounds and pronunciations of the words are again emphasized as keys to their meaning.]

Jim: Would you have some sort of final comment on the stones or the site in general?

George: Well, the stones felt much better this time than they did the first time.

Joel: Why is that? What was it about those stones several months ago that's so different now?

George: Maybe because it's already been said and done and now it's concentrating on something else.

[Comments are made of the fact that George is now "tuning in" beyond the blood element and concentrating on the community itself. Joel Martin then makes a parallel to the musical *Brigadoon*, a legendary town where the people would not—could not—leave their ancient community and so time literally stood still for them. That was the feeling George Anderson had when he "saw" the site in North Salem, southern New Hampshire, that time stood still.]

Oddly enough, this final thought of time standing still seemed to home in on a strong feeling of Jim Knusch's. During the many visits to the Hill, he experienced the feeling that the ancient residents were still there. Certainly their essences were as strong as ever. One could almost expect to visit the site one day and see maybe just for one hour, the small thriving community at work, the constructions fresh and new, activities going on. After beholding this sight, the site would fade and return to its present state.

In a follow-up session with George Anderson, one major element of what he "saw" during the radio show/videotaping was expanded upon. This major element was almost totally missed as an important factor of the psychometry. During the session George saw what appeared to him to be lines resembling telephone poles. Since no explanation for these lines came forth at the time, he interpreted them as possible symbols for lines of communication or as psychic links among the contemporary inhabitants.

Since that date, more research has been done by various members of the Mystery Hill staff, including research in the area of written communication through the ages. Ogham script is one of the oldest and most widespread forms of written communication. Variations of Ogham and similar forms of writing have been found etched in stone in the American West, in sections of Europe, and in small sections of southern New England. In the museum/artifact room at Mystery Hill is the Beltane stone. Dr. Barry Fell has labeled this one item (which now exists in two pieces) as perhaps "the most important inscription in North America." Significantly, this is an inscription that refers to a particular date. On the stone are carved Ogham symbols for "Day 39," symbols resembling, yet predating Roman numerals. The ancient Celts celebrated Beltane, their great May Day festival, on the 39th day of the year (their year begins on the day of the spring equinox). In 45 B.C., Julius Caesar changed the calendar, setting the "new" spring equinox on March 25, with the year beginning January 1. But that was in ancient Europe; in what is now New England the "old" spring equinox remained as May 1. Mark Feldman, in his book *The Mystery Hill Story*, believes that the Beltane stone must have been inscribed about the time of Christ.

Could George have picked up on one of these ancient inscribers, a contemporary of whoever carved the Beltane stone?

After the radio program, George was asked to tune in to the same stones used during the taping and then jot down any symbols, characters, shapes, images, or writing of any kind. The symbols and characters filled two pages and included a combination of what could be interpreted as Ogham, Micmac, and English. Not being a trained epigraphist, George most likely saw various shapes and forms and simply transcribed them as best he could. Interestingly, several characters could be translated as: "Tremble or Earthquake," "20 + idols + a dwelling of some sort, or a 'House of 20 idols,'" "Make an offering," "At present time," "A grassy field," "Seeing [into the future?]" and the letter G.

What is significant about the letter G? A carved stone exists on the site, outside the outer perimeter (containing the astronomical alignments); on it is carved something that resembles a capital G. This stone, appropriately called the "G Stone," refers to the sun god Bel. Bel was probably their supreme deity, quite possibly the primary reason for the choice of that particular tract of land and their construction of such a temple.

More extensive study needs to be done in the psychic exploration of America's Stonehenge. One could not realistically expect any more than fragments of this ancient civilization to be revealed in a few relatively simple sessions and several isolated tries by people not even in touch with each other. Yet psychic exploration of this enigmatic place in North Salem goes on, and hopefully will continue. Sometimes the researchers at Mystery Hill receive information from unexpected sources, such as this letter that appeared in *The Psychic Journal*, in which a woman named Jeannette described her visit to America's Stonehenge:

In spite of the other visitors coming and going, I decided to sit quietly for a few minutes on one of the old stones near the Oracle Chamber and Sacrificial Table and see if a bit of meditation would produce anything interesting.

With a thank-you to my own guides and any other spirits involved, I asked if there was a message that could be given to me. Sitting quite still, with my eyes closed for only moments, I was led to open my eyes and look up, ahead and slightly to my right. There on the flat area known as the "Sacrificial Table Viewing Ramp" I saw or received the impression of a tremendous block of translucent, or perhaps even transparent, shining gray granite. I mean probably thirty feet tall and ten to fifteen feet wide! Yet not square-cut and rock-hard as is usual with granite. Somehow its quality was expressed as power rather than hardness.

As mentioned earlier, I do not "see" things clearly so I can tell you little more than that about the appearance of the great [angel-nature Spirit] who is responsible for this area, but the "conversation" in mental concepts was quite clear. When I asked for a name, I was told Astonadai (as-to-na-da-a).

I asked how the people came to choose "his" area for this extensive construction. He indicated that they were led by their guides and the nature forces to this spot because of the innate power that was there. Just as evidence points, at Chartres Cathedral in France and many other sites, to the fact that the builders and oftentimes people long before them had known a spot to be "sacred ground."

According to Astonadai it was a combination of the rocks themselves. The way in which they lay (possibly in relationship to the center of the earth, but this was not entirely clear), and the relationship to the magma (or some similar power source from the earth itself), made this spot a chosen one. I have no idea if this same set of circumstances applies in other cases.

At that time two adults came close behind me and two pre-teen boys came toward me on the right side and it was impossible for me to maintain the contact. With a hasty thank-you and real regret at such a brief contact, I let the "vision" fade, but I will never forget the tremendous force that I felt as I chatted with the great nature spirit Astonadai.

America's Stonehenge is open to the public on weekends in April and November, and daily from May 1 through October 31. It is located at Mystery Hill, North Salem, New Hampshire, just off Route 111. Physicist or psychic, or just an ordinary person, you are welcome to visit. Who know? You, too, just might have a vision of mankind's history in the place where time stands still.

An Encounter in Fayette County

Stan Gordon first began to research UFO sightings and other strange phenomena when he was ten years old. Since 1965 he has conducted firsthand investigations into thousands of weird and unusual incidents taking place across his home state of Pennsylvania. Now even law-enforcement agencies and the news media refer cases to him.

The following amazing story, which is fully documented and which Stan Gordon personally investigated, is one of the oddest encounters ever recorded. All the names and places are real, with the exception of the Meacham family.

This was more than an encounter of the third kind—it was one step beyond. . . .

In 1970 Stan Gordon began the first of three UFO-research organizations that he would organize in Pennsylvania over many years. Individuals from various scientific and technical fields were needed to interpret data and to examine any physical evidence. Therefore the group had a number of research specialists on its volunteer staff.

As an electronic technician with a special interest in radio communications, Gordon already had a major radio-monitoring system in his Greensburg, Pennsylvania, home, which would serve as a base of operations. A two-way-radio network was organized so that direct contact could be maintained with field investigators, to send them to the site of ongoing incidents. The group acquired Geiger counters, metal detectors, and other research gear necessary for gathering data. A twenty-four-hour UFO hotline, already in operation, became even more active as the news media began to let the public know about the newly organized team.

The members became quite experienced at conducting witness interviews and gathering physical samples. But no matter how well-organized they became, they were unprepared for the siege of phenomena grasping sections of Pennsylvania during the summer of 1973. While the United States and many other parts of the world experienced a major outbreak of unexplained UFO activity, it seemed that Pennsylvania had been targeted for an onslaught of occurrences. During this UFO flap, more than six hundred UFO cases were reported.

But besides the UFO encounters, a more mysterious series of events occurred that made UFO history. Residents of the Pacific Northwest and Canada had for years reported encounters with giant, hairy, long-armed, apelike creatures that walked upright like humans—usually called "Bigfoot" or "Sasquatch"—but Pennsylvanians rarely ever heard of such things. But during the summer months of 1973, the largest number of Bigfoot sightings on record to occur within a specific geographical area broke out in seven counties in southwestern Pennsylvania.

At the same time, Amish farmers living in the Pennsylvania Dutch Country of Lancaster County in the eastern part of the state were reporting that hairy giants were carrying off their ducks and geese. Field teams were being dispatched around the clock. The result was over 130 Bigfoot-related events that involved more than 250 eyewitnesses.

Physical evidence was found at the locations where the incidents occurred. In many cases, fresh footprints were found; casts made of the footprints showed not only the number of toes but also weight distribution, bone structure, and muscle tone.

It was reported that dogs exhibited great fear when the creatures were close by. Many times investigators would arrive at a sighting within minutes. They would be amazed to see normally ferocious dogs standing or lying motionless as though paralyzed, not barking, not even letting out a whimper. Many times dogs, and occasionally other small animals such as rabbits, cats, and chickens, would be found torn limb from limb in the areas the creatures purportedly frequented.

During the 1973 Pennsylvania outbreak, and in a number of subsequent cases, well-documented incidents occurred where both a UFO and Bigfoot were observed at the same place, at the same time, by more than one witness. But none of them were as incredible as the following:

The events of October 25, 1973, were already generating quite a bit of excitement. Over a dozen UFO reports had been called in to Stan Gordon's UFO hotline. Early that morning, state and local police, as well as civilians, were reporting bright blue and red glowing lights moving erratically in the sky near Philipsburg. A bright red sphere with a long tail flew across the sky near Rillton. Later that evening, witnesses near Latrobe spotted three multicolored objects zigzagging across the sky.

At 10:30 P.M. Stan Gordon answered the telephone yet again. This time the caller was a state trooper from the Uniontown state-police barracks in Fayette County. He was shaken by an incident that he had just investigated and which he felt needed special attention. He gave Gordon a quick run-down and then passed the phone to twenty-two-year-old Stephen Meacham, the main witness, who was also at the police station.

Meacham was very upset and highly emotional. He had seen a ball of light drop slowly from the sky on his father's farm on the Vances Mill-Bute road in North Union Township, a rural area outside the city of Uniontown. The object landed in a pasture. He and two neighbor boys who went to investigate the light caught sight of two huge hairy creatures in the field at the same time. Stephen had fired a 30.06 rifle at them, with no effect.

When the officer arrived to investigate, he saw a large glowing area where the huge sphere had apparently been resting. As he and Stephen continued to search for evidence, they realized that something was following them as they walked. The men panicked, certain that the creatures were still in the area.

This was a situation that demanded an immediate on-scene investigation. A field team was quickly assembled and equipment was checked out. Radiation counters, searchlights, and tape recorders were tested. The team consisted of George E. Lutz, a former Air Force officer and pilot; David Smith, a science teacher and Westmoreland County's civil-defense radiation officer; Dennis Smeltzer, a sociology student; David Baker, a professional photographer and paramedic; and Stan Gordon.

The Uniontown area was a fifty-minute drive from Greensburg, so plans were made to meet at a mall there after midnight. The team assembled at 12:45 A.M. Friday, about three hours and forty-five minutes after the initial sighting, and met Stephen Meacham and his father, Frank. Stephen was checked carefully with radiation detection gear, since he and the trooper had stepped into the luminous area. Only normal background readings were evident. The small caravan then proceeded toward the Meacham farm, about fifteen minutes away. The area looked familiar to the researchers; two years previously, another strange incident involving a UFO and its occupants had been reported at another farm just down the road.

In the farmhouse, while they waited for additional witnesses involved in the sighting, Stephen Meacham explained the incident in detail:

It was about nine o'clock Thursday night that Stephen and his wife were driving their pickup truck down the dirt lane toward his family's house. They saw a strange light in the sky, like a big red ball.

When they reached the house, Stephen saw that his mother and his younger sisters were out on the porch, looking at the light. Stephen thought the red object appeared to be hovering about one hundred feet up.

"It looked as big as our barn, maybe larger," Stephen said.

The family watched it for about five more minutes, then called a family on the other side of the hill to ask if they could see it. Their neighbors went outside and immediately reported that the red ball was visible from their property. (Actually, a total of about fifteen people in the valley observed the object.) Stephen then drove down to the neighbors' house to have a look at the object from there.

"I looked up in the sky and it started to come down real slow, and it landed in my dad's field."

Two young neighbor boys accompanied Stephen back to his father's farm. As they pulled up to the Meacham house, the trio commented that it seemed like every dog in the valley was barking and upset. Stephen ran into the house and grabbed a box of ammunition, along with a 30.06 rifle. The box contained five rounds of ammo; the first two, unknown to Stephen at the time, were tracers (flares). He placed an extra bullet in his pocket and returned outside. Before he boarded his truck, he heard a loud whirring noise, like that of a lawn mower, and a crying sound, like a baby wailing in the distance. But he could not determine the sources of the sounds.

Stephen drove up a dirt road to the pasture area, parking the truck at an angle so that the headlights would give him and the boys light as they walked up the long slope toward the field. But as they began their walk, they noticed that the headlights appeared to be dimming, as if some force were draining them of power.

"We walked up in the field and, coming up over the horizon, we saw a dome-shaped bubble object, slightly flattened on the bottom. Instead of being red, now it was bright white. It was just sitting there, illuminating the field around it, and it sounded like a lawn mower running. It looked about one hundred feet in diameter."

The trio stood about 250 feet from the object, amazed at what they were seeing. All this time they still heard the sound of a baby crying, only now it was louder and apparently much closer. Then one of the boys yelled and pointed to the right. Seventy-five feet away, something was moving along the fence line. The barbed-wire fence, made of railroad ties partly buried in the ground, was about six feet tall. The group watched in shock as two huge figures slowly walked in their direction. At first Stephen thought they were bears, but he soon realized they were unlike anything he had ever come across before. They were apelike creatures with long arms that almost touched the ground—and they were two feet higher than the fenceposts were!

"The first creature was huge, eight or nine feet tall. The other one was smaller, maybe seven feet. The arms were so long they almost touched their feet. As they walked, they whined to each other, like a crying noise.

These things were brown, really furry, with long fur hanging down."

The hair looked very dirty and matted. The eyes were about the size of half-dollars, and they glowed bright green. The creatures seemingly had no necks, and no other physical features could be determined. But the hairy giants walked very stiff-legged, almost mechanically. The taller of the two creatures seemed to be leading the way, taking long strides as it followed the fence line. When it reached a fencepost it would whine as if signaling the second creature to come forward. When the second creature reached the post, the larger one would proceed to the next post position.

The shock of seeing all this was too much for one of the boys. Frightened, he ran from the field back to the truck. His brother yelled to Stephen to shoot at the creatures, who were still moving toward them.

Stephen took the safety off his gun and fired a tracer bullet over their heads. He then shot a second tracer, at which time the larger creature turned toward it, lifted its right arm, and seemed to touch it. At that exact moment the huge glowing object that had been sitting in the field suddenly vanished. The humming sound stopped as well.

Stephen commented, "It was just like you were suddenly in another world. The dogs suddenly stopped barking, and all of the other sounds stopped."

Both creatures turned around and followed the fence line back toward the woods. Stephen fired three rounds of regular ammo at them. He was sure he hit the larger one, since he heard a plopping sound, like a bullet hitting water. The creatures turned glowing eyes on him as he shot at them, but never changed pace. They gave no indication of being injured by the gunshot blasts. Stephen and the remaining boy retreated from the field and ran down to the truck.

When they reached it, they saw that the headlights were now very dim, as if giving off only candlepower. By this point, Stephen was badly frightened and did not want to leave his family in their home. He picked up his mother and sisters and drove everyone to the neighbors' house, where they decided to report the incident to the state police. The call was placed to the Uniontown barracks, and an officer arrived about 9:45 P.M. to question Stephen.

The young trooper was quite skeptical. "I'm here to investigate the flying saucer," he said, grinning.

Stephen, feeling uneasy, told him to just forget it. "You wouldn't believe it anyhow." But the trooper stated that he *had* to investigate the case, since, the night before, a man had reported two apelike creatures just over the mountain.

Stephen and the trooper drove to the field, the trooper aiming his lights on the area where the UFO had landed. The object was gone, but the spot was strangely glowing. Stephen and one of the boys had noticed this when the object initially disappeared, but didn't take the time to investigate. The trooper estimated this circular glow to be about 150 feet in diameter. The illumination extended about a foot off the ground, and was bright enough to reveal the details of small plants within the circle. The officer shone his flashlight into the glowing area, and the beam was hardly noticeable. The temperature was slightly warmer in the glowing area, and both men noticed the cattle and horses in the field were careful to avoid the spot.

As he examined the site, the trooper was incredulous. "This is really something," he told Stephen, now eager to continue his search for evidence.

"I don't get paid for being brave," Stephen said. "I'm not going any further."

162

The officer realized that Stephen was quite scared. He suggested that they go back to the barracks and call the UFO center in Greensburg. As they walked toward the car, they heard the sound of heavy footsteps behind them in the woods.

"We heard two steps like timber cracking," Stephen reported later. "We were about fifty feet away from the police car at the time, and I told the officer that I just couldn't take this anymore. I had one bullet left, so I loaded the gun and pulled the chamber closed. I could see that the trooper was beginning to sweat. He shone his flashlight toward the sound—the largest of the two creatures was standing ten feet away in front of us! The officer made a loud gasping sound, and his flashlight shook. I shot directly into the chest of the creature. It swayed backward, then came right at the fence. We could hear the wire ping. We ran back to the patrol car. The officer locked all four doors hurriedly, then ripped his pants trying to get out his car keys. He seemed in shock; he kept revving the engine, and the car was going in a circle. I yelled at him, and that seemed to bring him to his senses."

"What was that?" the trooper asked pointlessly.

"I don't know," said Stephen. "That's why I called you."

They drove down to Route 51, where the trooper stopped his car. "Oh, my God, I can't believe I saw that thing." After regaining his composure, he got on the radio and called the barracks.

The dispatcher answered. He asked the trooper, in a teasing manner, "Did you find any spacemen?"

"There is something definitely there," the trooper replied.

When Stephen and the officer arrived at the state-police barracks, more troopers were waiting on the sidewalk. Inside, the police offered Stephen coffee before taking him into a separate room; the trooper was put into another room. After they were interviewed separately, a decision was made to call Stan Gordon.

It was 1:30 A.M. when Stan's team made its way up the dirt road that led to the field, to meet up with Stephen and his father, Frank. The young boys who had been involved in the sighting were also now present; though they were asked to remain in the truck until the team returned. Stephen wanted to take his rifle, but took his dog instead. "Thank God that decision was made," said Stan. As they walked toward the field, they looked for more evidence to substantiate the sightings. Stan switched on a tape recorder.

The glowing area was no longer visible. Radiation levels were carefully checked, but only normal background readings were detected. As before, a number of cows in the field stayed around the perimeter of the reported landing site, but would not venture into it.

At 1:45 A.M. Stephen and his father yelled that suddenly, for several seconds, their farmhouse (about 700 feet away from the field) had become bright as daylight. They all turned to look.

"It was all illuminated in white. And then it just went out." Stephen saw a big white ball encapsulate the house. The mysterious light source vanished as suddenly as it had appeared. George Lutz, the retired Air Force officer and former pilot, and Frank Meacham took a look around the house, but everything appeared normal.

"Hear those dogs down there?" Stephen said, referring to a loud cacophony of barking which had suddenly erupted. "Those dogs are barking like crazy. I didn't see anybody come up in a car. Did you?"

"No," said Stan. "The light went out too fast."

The search continued in the field. The group walked toward the location along the fence where the creatures had been seen. They noticed that a lone bull in the pasture above them seemed more interested in a remote part of the Meacham field, away from the group. The men thought that strange; they were causing a small commotion, and had the bull been exhibiting normal behavior, he would have turned his attention to the group.

Stephen pointed toward the area where the creatures had been.

"Is that an electric fence?" Stan asked.

"No. Just a barbed-wire fence. The electrical fence is above it, though, and it's on. I don't know whether they could feel it from there or not."

Stephen's dog suddenly became excited, sniffing and tracking ahead. It stopped several times and gazed toward a corner of the woods.

"I'd loaded the gun; didn't realize I'd used tracers—they explode—then I saw them. They were brownish-gray, long hair, and their arms were almost touching their feet. And when I shot that first tracer, one of them went 'ahhh'—a high pitched call or scream. Then it stuck its hand out, after I fired the second tracer, and the UFO light just popped and went out.

"When I fired the second tracer, they turned around and did a real slow walk back. I had three shots more and I figured I might as well shoot them."

"And you think you did hit them?" Stan asked.

"I had to hit them. But it didn't faze them. They kept the same gait. They never hurried.

"I'm just like most people. I never believed in this shit before. I feel I have to see it to believe it. I believe it now. Believe me, I believe it now."

They all felt a little uneasy.

Stephen continued to point out where things had happened. "They were following all along here. We walked right through this opening up here."

Stan instructed Dennis Smeltzer, "See if you can find any signs or broken branches."

As they walked, George Lutz noticed that Stephen was rubbing his face and head.

"Are you dizzy?" George asked.

Instead of replying, Stephen shook back and forth as though he was going to pass out. So George Lutz, on one side, and Stephen's father, on the other, grabbed Stephen to keep him from falling. Suddenly Stephen began to breathe very heavily and growl like a wild animal. He furiously threw back his arms; George and Frank fell to the ground.

Stephen's dog ran toward him, barking, as if he was going to attack his own master. Instead, Stephen turned on the dog, and the animal ran off, whimpering.

"Bring your camera!" someone yelled to Dave Baker.

Stephen's growling alarmed his father, who tried to calm him. "Hey, son. C'mon, Stephen."

Stephen's only reply was another strong growl. He ran ahead of them, swinging his arms and making loud inhuman noises. George Lutz and Stephen's father screamed at him to come back, that they were going to take him back to the truck. After additional seconds, which felt like hours, Stephen let out a blood-curdling scream, followed by three more low growls. Suddenly things began to go wrong for the rest of the investigative team:

Dennis Smeltzer called out, "Stan, I'm feeling a little light-headed. I think I'm going to faint."

"I'll be right with you, Denny," called Dave Baker. He and David Smith went over to see what was wrong with Smeltzer, who looked quite pale. Baker was having trouble breathing as well.

Stephen Meacham suddenly collapsed, facedown, into the manure-covered field and started moaning. George Lutz ran to him, followed by Frank Meacham.

"Get back," Stephen warned. "Get out of here."

"Son, you're all right," his father said soothingly. "There's nothing here now. You just tripped over some wood."

"Get away, get away," Stephen yelled. "There's something here... Don't... don't..."

George Lutz tried to coax him up. "Let's go out this way, Stephen."

"Stay there!" Stephen shouted. His voice had changed and was very commanding. "Don't come down here."

"Okay," Frank Meacham agreed. "Just watch the barbed wire."

During this exchange, the entire group noticed a strong smell, like that of rotten eggs, permeating the area. It was a sickening odor and it affected them all. They decided to return to the vehicles and lifted Stephen from the ground and got him to walk a few steps.

"Feeling any better?" Frank Meacham asked. "Close your eyes and just walk—I'll hold you."

"No, no... I saw a man," whispered Stephen, "all dressed in black. He was carrying a sickle or a scythe. He came..."

"What did you see?" Stan asked, confused.

"A man. A man with a black robe and a black hat with a scythe over his back. He told me the world... he told me if man doesn't straighten up, the world's going to perish. But he said there's one man that can save the world—the man's here. He said the man's here."

"C'mon," urged Frank. "Let's get out of here."

"Yeah," George Lutz agreed. "Let's go down to the car. I feel chills."

"Does anyone else feel light-headed?" asked David Smith as they trudged along. Stephen, who stood 6'2" and weighed about 250 pounds, was difficult to move and they could only manage a few steps at a time.

"Me," said Dave Baker.

"Not me," said Stan. "But I sure did smell something."

"My ankles are killing me," grumbled Stephen as he stumbled along.

"Should we let him rest?" asked Dave Baker.

"I wanted to kill something," said Stephen. "Somebody, something—I don't know what it was. My hands, my whole body feels numb."

"Relax your hands," instructed George Lutz. "Just think about something else." He examined Stephen's hands: they were clenched so tightly that his fingers could not be pried open.

"Something told me..." Stephen sighed. "I was told nothing could hurt me." Then he realized that others in the group were not well. When he expressed concern for their feelings, the others felt Stephen was finally coming out of his trance or fit.

As they continued to walk, Frank Meacham handed his son the glasses that had fallen off his face when he collapsed. To his surprise, Stephen exclaimed, "Whose glasses are these? I see fine."

The men eventually reached the vehicles but didn't tell the young boys, who were still sitting in one of the trucks, what had taken place. Stan's group took Frank Meacham aside and questioned him as to whether his son had ever experienced any states similar to what they had just witnessed. He said that this was the first time anything like this had ever happened. Once inside the car, the team continued their discussion.

"I felt like I just walked up the side of a mountain," complained Dave Baker. "I couldn't breathe."

They all were alarmed by the other strange events they had witnessed, but Stephen Meacham's behavior was extraordinary. During the drive back, they played portions of tape recordings made during Stephen's "attack." The chilling sounds coming from Stephen were more animal than human. And several group members noted that the ultimate scream, the one Stephen made before he passed out, was incredibly similar to sounds recently captured on tape by a Pennsylvanian who claimed to have seen and recorded "Bigfoot." Stan and his group were quickly convinced that there was no easy explanation, and they were deeply concerned for Stephen's well-being. Since they could not rule out the possibility that he might be harmful to himself or others, the group felt professional assistance was necessary. The person they decided had the best credentials to enter this case was eminent psychiatrist Berthold E. Schwarz, M.D., now of Vero Beach, Florida.

Dr. Schwarz had graduated from Dartmouth College and Dartmouth Medical School and received his degree from New York University, College of Medicine. He was a fellow in psychiatry at the Mayo Foundation, a diplomat of the American Board of Psychiatry and Neurology, a fellow of the American Psychiatric Association and the Academy of Medicine of New Jersey, and a member of many other highly regarded medical associations. His special interest, however, was unexplained phenomena, and he'd written numerous articles and books on a variety of such topics.

Dr. Schwarz took great interest in the Meacham case when he was contacted. During the initial phone conversation, he was given full details as to what had transpired, and in turn he instructed Stan in what to do until he arrived. He volunteered to drive at his own expense from his home in Montclair, New Jersey, to Pennsylvania.

Since Dr. Schwarz could not arrive in Greensburg until November 1, George Lutz and Stan Gordon went back to Uniontown for a follow-up interview with Stephen Meacham. On October 27, the three of them met around the dining table at his father's house. Stephen remembered in detail all of the events that had occurred the night before—up to the point when George asked how he felt. Stephen recalled nothing about his fit.

In the middle of the questions, another frightening episode occurred. Stephen was asked if he had any idea why the UFO and the creatures were seen together. He again began to rub his head, did not reply, and started to breathe heavily.

George and Stan screamed at him, afraid he would have another fit.

The screaming did the trick; George and Stan realized they apparently had to avoid certain questions. But the real mystery was why the pursuit of certain information seemed to cause this response. It was another aspect of the case which would be left to Dr. Schwarz.

They also learned that earlier that day, the state trooper who had initially investigated the incident had returned to the farm to look for evidence. In the daylight, George and Stan found the grass in the Meacham field trampled, and the barbed-wire fence broken where the creature had hit it.

The trooper was not the only visitor to the farm the day after the sighting. A reporter from the local Uniontown newspaper wanted an interview. Apparently the Uniontown state police had released information on the sighting (without mentioning the trooper) to the news media. The reporter was quite skeptical, but he asked Stephen to take him to the location of the shooting. As they entered the area, the reporter remarked that if Stephen really had shot at the creatures, then there should be some bullet casings around. The reporter looked down and found three casings under his feet, and Stephen bent over to pick up the other two!

When Dr. Schwarz arrived, he was given full access to the many hours of taped interviews with the subjects involved, as well as written reports. He personally interviewed Stephen, his parents, the two young boys and their family, as well as the state trooper and members of the investigating team. During subsequent interviews with Stephen, Schwarz determined that even though he did not have much of an interest in reading, Stephen was highly intelligent and could give detailed accounts of experiences he had been through during various stages of his life. Schwarz also learned that Stephen had no previous knowledge of subjects such as UFOs or the occult. Meacham, in fact, was quite skeptical of stories people had told over the years about local sightings of strange lights in the sky.

Dr. Schwarz, after conducting a lengthy study of the case, wrote a comprehensive summary on the psychiatric aspects as it related to Stephen. This account, which appeared in the Vol. 20, No. 1, 1974, edition of *Flying Saucer Review*, published in England, presented information that substantiated that the sighting had likely occurred as reported:

> The unusual circumstances, and the fact that various segments of events at different times were witnessed by thirteen (or more) people, indicate the reality of the experiences. In all instances it seemed that Stephen and the others were truthful. There was no evidence of dishonesty, lying, sociopathic behavior, use of hallucinogenic drugs or alcohol, in connection with this experience or previously. The reports of the various witnesses, family members, and neighbors were compatible. Part of the action was recorded as it was happening. Specifically, it would seem in reality that there were lights which

were first low in the sky and which then descended to nearly land, or hovered low above the ground, and which had an associated lawn-mower sound; that the UFO might have dimmed the truck lights; that the brightness of the UFO's lights inflamed the eyes of two witnesses; and that the action and the stench associated with the creatures caused presumed behavioral reactions for the people involved and for dogs, horses, a bull, and cattle. Stephen's story was essentially the same whether given to the UFO study group, the trooper, or to me. It was fully corroborated by independent interviews of the other witnesses by the study group and by me.

Dr. Schwarz felt that Stephen had experienced a "fugue" state during the final incident in the field. The *Encyclopedia and Dictionary of Medicine and Nursing* defines a fugue state as "transitory abnormal behavior marked by aimless wandering and some alteration of consciousness, usually but not always followed by amnesia."

Dr. Schwarz further felt that Stephen's acute fugue was out of context for him. A study of his past life revealed no evidence of any previous similar dissociative, disoriented behavior, nor any character traits like sleep-walking, sleep-talking, fainting, amnesia, or trancelike states. Nor was there any medical explanation.

The information derived from Stephen, his parents, his neighbors, and several physicians indicated that the fugue was a specific reaction to the UFO-creatures experience! Unfortunately, for all his research, Dr. Schwarz was no closer to finding an answer.

The Fayette County case became one of the first of many incidents over the years linking extraterrestrial spacecraft to unknown zoological animals. It became a procedure of Stan Gordon's to keep in touch with witnesses who had reported these dual sightings. He wanted to determine why some of these people seemed to experience "repeated" phenomena of various types after an initial experience. It was during one of the follow-up sessions with Stephen, many years after the 1973 incident, that Stan was in for another shock.

During their visit, Stan and George were discussing with Stephen the pros and cons of using hypnotic regression to fill in missing time events related to UFO experiences.

"Why would you want to hypnotize me now?" Stephen asked. "You already did that."

"When?"

"A couple weeks after the sighting," Stephen replied.

George Lutz and Stan Gordon were stunned. They had never done any hypnosis on Stephen, on the recommendation of Dr. Schwarz. And Schwarz had told Stephen directly, during one of his interviews, that hypnosis would not be used at that time. Stephen didn't believe in hypnosis anyway; but Schwarz, in his report, gave a more important reason why he counseled against hypnosis:

Superficially, hypnotic studies, including an attempt at regression (or a sodium pentothal interview), might seem attractive. But they were contraindicated because during his interview with the study group, as well as with me, Stephen frequently gave indications of becoming entranced while recalling certain aspects of the creature/Man-in-Black sequence. He had to be forcefully called back to consciousness and there was a clear-cut danger of violence under the prevailing conditions.

Stephen said that about a week after one of the many interviews at his home in 1973 (with Stan, George, and Dr. Schwarz), two men showed up on his doorstep. They wanted to interview him about his UFO/creature sighting. Stephen had always thought that these men were part of Stan's research team. In fact, he thought that one of these men was George Lutz in his Air Force uniform.

One man was about six feet tall, with dark short hair. He was dark-complexioned and had stocky arms and big hands. The other man was dressed in a military uniform; Stephen recalled that he was a major. They sat down at the dining-room table and asked Stephen to recall the events of the night of October 25, 1973. When Stephen completed his report, the officer opened up a briefcase full of papers and photos.

"Stephen, you're not crazy," he said. "This is what we have."

He pulled out numerous photographs of unidentified flying objects and asked Stephen to point out any photos similar to what he had seen. Then he pulled out more showing Bigfoot creatures, just like what Stephen had shot at. One picture, which Stephen clearly recalled, was that of a creature climbing over a fence, carrying a pig under its arm. The photo had been taken in Georgia, according to the officer.

The man in the uniform asked for permission to hypnotize Stephen, who consented. Stephen remembered the man holding a large ring in front of his face and quickly repeating certain words over and over again. He remembered them telling him, "This won't hurt you."

Before they left they thanked Stephen for his help and stated: "Don't let it bother you. In time, it will go away. We will be in contact with you."

Whoever Stephen's visitors were, they were not members of Stan Gordon's investigative team. The Air Force claimed no knowledge of conducting such an interview, since they had been out of public-level UFO investigations since 1969. Whether the men were indeed government personnel or just impersonators, they apparently were aware of some cases that connected UFOs with Bigfoot-like creatures. In fact, subsequent cases have proved to Stan Gordon that either the Air Force or a government agency *is* involved in handling UFO investigations and most definitely knows about the UFO/creature connection.

The incident on that October night in 1973 had a traumatic effect on those involved. One of the boys who witnessed the phenomena had to be taken to a local hospital the next day and given tranquilizers. Nightmares kept him from sleeping. Not long after the incident, the investigating state trooper resigned from the police force and moved out west. Some sources close to him felt that this event greatly affected his life.

Stephen Meacham, who had neither interest nor belief in psychic phenomena, began to have bizarre experiences that nearly unraveled his life. He seemed to be able to pick up on other people's thoughts. He experienced precognitive dreams and visions of major national tragedies before they occurred. He would tell friends and relatives about some of these things before they would occur. He had advance knowledge of the death of Natalie Wood, and of the crash of a Japanese commercial airliner, as well as of other incidents. These psychic events continued for many years and disrupted his life quite often. They finally began to decrease in intensity during the mid-1980's.

"I wouldn't recommend anyone going through this experience," said Stephen. "You go through so much torment and hell for the first couple of years. Eventually you learn to stabilize yourself, but there are so many sleepless nights trying to figure it out. I didn't want to know or see any of these things. Why did it happen to me? If I could figure it out, I would feel a lot better."

Unfortunately, no one has an answer. Perhaps the mysterious government men, who promised to stay in touch, will come back and explain it all. Or perhaps they know but aren't telling. There are rumors that there is an extra floor in the Pentagon, with thousands of files documenting cases just like Stephen Meacham's. . . .

The Wonderworker of the Santa Fe Trail

Maurice Schwalm is a psychic consultant in Kansas City, where he had his own radio show, The World of Psychic Phenomena. *Since 1970 he has investigated and reported on hundreds of haunted houses and actually photographed ghosts! He prefers to personally do on-site investigations and has traveled widely in search of the unknown.*

For this next story, Maurice Schwalm traveled to the caves and mountains of New Mexico, in search of an extraordinary man known as "The Hermit." Though the Hermit died over a hundred years ago, worshipers still make pilgrimages to the cave where his spirit is said to still work miracles. . . .

Under the council oak in Council Grove, Kansas, the first Indian treaty was signed on August 10, 1825, giving settlers the right to travel on what would be the first federal highway. Because Council Grove was now the jumping-off point for settlers traveling west, the town teemed with strangers. People didn't stay in one spot long enough for anyone to learn their names—and sometimes they used aliases if they had something to hide.

And so it was with Matteo Boccalini, who arrived in Council Grove in 1863. Matteo was known by various names, but after a while he was known only as "The Hermit."

This was not the usual cowboy or settler passing through town. Matteo, dressed in the robes of a Franciscan friar, had an imposing white beard and walked using a staff. It was believed that this unusual new arrival had come from Rome—from the Vatican, no less—where he had been a papal secretary before his expulsion on political matters. The fact that he could speak five languages fluently proved he was no ordinary man. And he told the most impossible tales: that he had lived in a cave in Missouri after escaping from Italy; that he was pursued by mysterious persons, including Jesuits who were intent on murdering him; that he was involved in a duel over a woman . . . was descended from Justinian the Great . . . had campaigned with Garibaldi . . .

Still wearing his robes, Matteo again took up residence in a cave, outside the city limits, where he erected a cross. People who lived down the hillside from him could hear him strumming a mandolin. Matteo liked to sit on a projecting ledge at the mouth of his rocky and isolated retreat and sing, sometimes vespers, sometimes Neapolitan songs, as well as soft airs of his native island of Capri. For five months the Hermit administered sacraments to the people of the Santa Fe Trail and wandered from one Indian tribe to another, teaching the Gospel.

All of Matteo's attempts to convert the Kaw Indians failed. Not only were they not impressed with his words and songs, the Indians regarded him as "bad medicine." There were local legends about a bearded white man whose presence would signal the beginning of the end for their tribal life.

The townspeople as well as the Indians were suspicious of Matteo and found him very enigmatic. His outlandish stories and living quarters were the subject of gossip. He told people he was the son of a noble family from the island of Capri, off the coast of southern Italy. Matteo even had photos of himself in the garb of an aristocrat. He explained that he had been selected to be a papal secretary before leaving Italy, but his appointment had been opposed by the Jesuits—rather strongly—and he had felt it expedient to leave Italy abruptly. He had come to the frontier—possibly via South America—apparently without a formal religious commission to evangelize. He also kept a mysterious diary that no one was allowed to see.

Convinced that someone from Rome was close to finding him, and feeling that he'd been identified by this shadowy follower, Matteo again packed up and left. He asked for and received a letter of introduction from the commander of the garrison at Council Grove. The letter of recommendation stated that he was a person of good character and a missionary to the Indians, that he preferred living in caves and subsisting entirely on vegetables.

This bizarre missive in hand, Matteo made contact with a wagon-train camp on May 28, 1863, so that he could join forces with them on the trip through to New Mexico. The wagon train was organized by Don Manuel Romero, who had the title *Mayordomo* and who was part-owner of one of the wagon trains that regularly plied the Santa Fe Trail.

Don Manuel agreed to allow Matteo to accompany them. He offered Matteo a ride in one of the wagons, but Matteo refused.

"All I want is the privilege of accompanying you to the mountains of the West. I prefer to walk, thank you, sir."

The surprised Don Manuel found Matteo a most unusual man—and thus began a close friendship between the two.

The Hermit ministered to all who were sick or in need of various sacraments along the trail. He refused to eat the various meat dishes provided during the journey. He never ate anything there, or while living with the Romero household when he arrived in New Mexico, other than a simple dish of *atol*. (*Atol* is a mush or gruel of Aztec origin, made from parched corn, commonly used by Spanish Americans up to the time of World War I.)

Before long, the Hermit was afraid the comfortable life with the Romeros would distract him from his mission, and despite his strong friendship with the family, he moved from Las Vegas, New Mexico, to a small village near Romeroville. There he found a natural cave in the east wall of a canyon. There he set up residence, and it was there, in the Catholic culture of the Southwest, that he finally flourished.

The Hermit spent most of his time in solitary meditation, but occasionally ministered to the poor and to the sick, and soon his reputation spread. Matteo treated the sick through potions and rubefacients (much in the manner of the famed Edgar Cayce, who prescribed medicines while in a trance). Matteo also helped his patients using other methods: sometimes with a laying-on of hands, hypnotism, materializing food and water, and telekinetically started fires.

As word of the miracle worker spread, crowds of people approached him, seeking healing. They pitched tents and windbreaks near the cave, hoping to see or even touch him. Soon Matteo found himself oppressively surrounded by people and he moved once more, this time to a mountaintop in, appropriately enough, the Sangre de Cristo (Blood of Christ) Mountains. It was located at the head of Gallinas Canyon, eighteen miles northwest of Las Vegas, New Mexico.

The mountain in question was already known as Owl's Peak but soon it became identified with Matteo and is now known as Hermit's Peak. From there, ten thousand feet high, he was able to survey the valleys below. At a point about three hundred feet below the eastern side of the peak, he selected a cave that provided him with shelter. He asked the men of the village to help him clean it up. When they had finished, he asked them to cover the front of the cave—creating for him the privacy of a cloistered cell—and leave only a tiny opening. This surprised the men, since it was not apparent how Matteo could enter and leave the cave under these circumstances.

As if reading their minds, he told them, "Do not worry. I have my ways and means of getting out of the cave."

Matteo's selection of the cave site near Las Vegas, New Mexico, may not have been totally arbitrary. There are many springs in the area that traditionally are thought to have medicinal value. According to legend, Montezuma, the Aztec king, settled there with his people. The Aztecs credited the springs with having magic powers related to the source and continuation of governmental powers. So it was from Las Vegas that Montezuma was led by an eagle to Mexico City, which is also built on water. The local Pueblo Indians maintained an eternal fire at the springs as well.

But the Hermit had little need for existing springs. As part of his settlement effort on the mountaintop, the Hermit was occasionally helped by a Don Margarito Romero and several of his men. Don Margarito pointed out to the Hermit that he would need a well. Matteo simply took his staff and struck the earth. Water gushed forth. That spring is still in existence. It has the peculiarity of rising up from the earth, only to be swallowed up by the ground just a few feet away.

It was on the mountaintop that the Hermit's many powers manifested themselves. There seemed no end to what he could do.

A group of pilgrims had come to worship with him. From his vantage point, he gestured to the hills near the village of Gallinas.

"There are many different kinds of minerals down there. There is much gold—gold veins as thick as *vigas* [beams]. However, it will be well into the future before the gold is discovered, and it will be strangers from afar who will discover it."

Matteo's prediction came to pass as prospectors, traveling the Santa Fe Trail, discovered gold in the hills. The area came to be known as Mineral Hill and was the site of several flourishing gold mines; the remains of abandoned gold mines can still be seen today.

Another story about the Hermit concerned a local peasant named Pablo, who was known as being rather arrogant. Pablo decided to travel up the mountain and see the Hermit. He was a musician who wanted to learn some new hymns, so he asked the Hermit if he would teach him a new one. Matteo agreed to teach him *"Corazón Santo"* (Sacred Heart). Pablo was not pleased at this announcement, since this was an ancient but well-known hymn, and he made fun of the Hermit's knowledge. Angry at being mocked, the Hermit told Pablo he would be severely punished for his attitude, and punished that very day.

Pablo mounted his horse and left, whistling happily as he rode away. As he was going down the mountain, a sudden cloudburst erupted and Pablo was struck and killed by a bolt of lightning.

Still more of the Hermit's powers came to light. One day Mr. and Mrs. Eulogio Ortega, who lived in the village of Gallinas, were on their way to attend Mass. The church, Our Lady of Sorrows, was several miles outside of town. On the road ahead of them they spotted a figure. They soon caught up with him and realized it was the Hermit, or, as he was known sometimes locally, El Solitario (the Lonely One). They offered him a ride to church but he

refused. He didn't need one, he said, but they had
better hurry or they'd be late for Mass.

The Ortegas went on their way, amused because
they were riding and he was walking and they felt that
they had plenty of time. However, when they arrived,
they saw El Solitario going up the steps to the church
ahead of them! By the time they parked the wagon and
took care of their horse and entered the church, the last
bell was ringing and Mass had already started.

Eventually Matteo felt he wanted to worship more
formally on his mountaintop hideaway. He asked the
families of the area, as well as the pilgrims who came to
see him, if they would help set up the fourteen stations
of the cross for his devotional use. They were only too
glad to help. After the stations were built, it became a
tradition, on the Fridays of Lent, to join Matteo in
observances.

One year, a young woman known as Feliz attended
with her little girl, Anita. The girl became restless and
asked to be excused to play. But her running took her
close to the edge of the cliff, where she slipped and fell,
landing on a ledge below. Hysterical, Feliz screamed
for help, but the ledge was not accessible. While people
scrambled for a solution and frantically tied ropes
together, suddenly Anita, with the Hermit at her side,
appeared on safe ground. No one knew how she had
been saved, and in fact the Hermit refused to give any
explanation.

On another occasion, Antonia, a pious woman from
Las Vegas, wished to visit the Hermit to obtain some
herbs and his blessing. Her neighbor Consuelo agreed
to accompany her, out of curiosity. Consuelo had heard
that the Hermit could read minds, and she wanted to
put him to the test. On the mountaintop, Antonia
received the herbs she requested and also a promise
that the Hermit would remember her and her family in

his prayers. Then he turned to Consuelo and said, "Please come with me, I want to show you something."

He led to her to another cave a short distance away. "Look in that cave," he instructed, "and tell me what you see. I hope your curiosity is satisfied."

Inside the cave was a rattlesnake, coiled and ready to strike. Consuelo ran away and the Hermit followed. "That's all you will see up here," he said. The message was that he wasn't running a magic show. What he did was for the benefit of others and was not to satisfy idle curiosity.

Every afternoon the Hermit had the habit of coming down from his mountaintop retreat to the Gallinas Canyon area, where he would spend time in prayer and meditation amid the canyon's natural beauty. Many pilgrims often accompanied the Hermit in his devotions and then would patiently wait for him to finish his meditation and pack up his case full of prayer books. Then they would offer to help him carry the heavy case back up the mountain.

On one particular occasion a young man named Hosea came to help the Hermit. When he approached the holy man, he saw the Hermit kneeling, reading from an open Bible. Hosea could see the pages turning, but something puzzled him. He walked closer and realized that the Hermit's hands were folded and not touching the Bible. There was no breeze, yet the pages were turning themselves!

Another time, a young boy named Willie went to the canyon to help the Hermit with his books. Young Willie was a difficult child and did not mind his parents; his mother hoped some good might come from his meeting the Hermit. This time, unlike others, Willie was allowed to carry the briefcase up the mountain. As they walked, Willie was puzzled because the briefcase kept getting heavier and heavier, and he complained to Matteo.

"*Perezo* [lazy one]," the holy man replied, "it is not the briefcase that is heavy, but your sins. And your sins are the ones that are weighing you down. Say an act of contrition and perhaps you will find some relief."

Willie did as he was told, and the briefcase lightened.

On at least two specific occasions involving food, the Hermit exhibited some unusual abilities. One day, a Mr. Atencio wished to go on a pilgrimage to the Hermit and he asked his wife to prepare some food, not only for his trip but also as an offering to the holy man. This was done, but only grudgingly after considerable discussion.

When Mr. Atencio arrived, he was greeted kindly. But when the food was offered, Matteo said, "This food was grudgingly prepared; however, I will accept it since you were so kind as to bring it to me!"

In another instance, a young boy, Aduardo, stole some apple pies from his mother and took them to the Hermit. The Hermit simply told him, "Take these pies back to your mother. And the next time you want to bring me something, please don't bring me anything that has been stolen!"

Frequently the Hermit lived parables rather than teaching them. The women of the village of Gallinas had the custom of baking bread in outside ovens. This bread was called "*pan de sábado*" (Sabbath bread). Anyone who needed bread had but to ask in the name of Jesus.

One particular woman, Anastacia, was known as being rather stingy. She saw the Hermit walking toward her house while she was baking, and she assumed that he was coming to ask for bread in the name of Jesus.

Instead of waiting for him to reach her, Anastacia went inside the house, picked up an already baked loaf, and stuffed it with rat poison. Then she took it outside. When the Hermit reached the house, she handed him the poisoned bread; he accepted it with a smile.

Later that afternoon, Anastacia's son Lucio came home from the fields. He took a loaf of freshly baked bread and ate it. Shortly afterward he fell extremely ill. Anastacia, horrified, realized Lucio must have eaten the poisoned bread intended for the Hermit—although she could not understand how that was possible. Lucio was very sick for days, but finally recovered.

That following Saturday, the Hermit came unbidden to call on her. He found Anastacia sad and repentant and she fell on her knees, begging for forgiveness. He quoted a rhyme to her:

"He who does a good deed benefits himself. He who does an evil deed does himself an injury."

After a few years in the Gallinas Canyon area, Matteo felt the pull of wanderlust yet again. He collected a few belongings and left his mountaintop retreat. Before he left, however, one of the things he did was to predict his own death.

It is thought that he wandered as far as San Antonio, Texas, before coming back to New Mexico. In the area of Old Mesilla, sometime around 1868, he again found a cave and resumed his ministry. There he befriended a Colonel Fountain, who was a close friend of the Romero family of Las Vegas and who had of course heard about the Hermit from them.

The Hermit never revealed his age to anyone, but it was thought that by this time he was at least seventy years old; Colonel Fountain certainly felt that Matteo was getting on in years and should have some way of signaling for help. After all, he was in a totally isolated area. Matteo finally agreed that he would light a fire at a certain time each day—a signal that he was alive and well on his mountaintop.

On one day in April 1869, no fire signal was seen. At first Colonel Fountain wasn't sure if the Hermit had gone on one of his wanderings or if something was truly wrong. When there was no signal the next day, and the next, Colonel Fountain organized a posse. On the mountaintop, lying prostrate in front of the cave, was Matteo's body, a dagger in his back.

The posse searched the area. All of Matteo's belongings were untouched, so perhaps robbery was not the motive. The body had not been scalped or otherwise mutilated, so Indians were not to blame. Matteo's death remained an unsolved mystery, unless one wanted to believe his enemies from Rome had finally caught up with him. . . .

The Hermit, though, lives on after death. A society devoted to his memory, known as La Sociedad del Ermitano (the Society of the Hermit), still exists today. Each year they spend the week prior to the Feast of the Holy Cross at the Hermit's cave. (The Feast is on September 14th.) Hermit's Peak is easy to reach; the cave is located on the east slope of the mountain, above the El Porveneer Hotel, seventeen miles northwest of Las Vegas, New Mexico, via Highway 65. By a strange coincidence, El Porveneer means "the one to come."

The Society lights bonfires in imitation of the Hermit's signals. There is singing and praying; occasionally they hold symbolic funerals, complete with graveside ceremonies, in his name. Sometimes the open graves are found the next day mysteriously filled. Often an ill devotee is healed by praying to the Hermit and many such minor miracles are common.

In 1898, a devotional group made a pilgrimage to the cave and took photos of themselves and the area. When the photos were developed, they were shocked to find that an image of Our Lady of Guadalupe had appeared in one of the pictures! They were sure that somehow the Hermit was responsible.

More recently, a priest from San Juan Church in Pueblo, New Mexico, held a mass at the cave. He and the parishioners were startled when, precisely at the end of the mass, a white dove suddenly appeared on the altar table. Doves are rarely seen at 10,000 feet.

In July of 1985, Maurice Schwalm, a psychic investigator from Missouri, traveled to the Hermit's cave dwelling in Kansas, which is not difficult to find and which is still accessible. In fact, the official historic tour brochure of Council Grove lists it simply as "No. 9, Hermit's Cave." The description in the brochure, however, makes no mention of the Hermit's powers.

Schwalm took several color Polaroid photos outside the cave; some strange objects materialized in one photograph. The picture showed some unusual objects outside the mouth of the cave, which of course were not there when Schwalm took the photo. In fact, Schwalm had difficulty understanding their significance: a circular white object and a smaller, irregularly curved yellow object.

Only later, when he researched the life of Matteo Boccalini, the wonderworker of the Santa Fe Trail, did Schwalm understand what these objects were: a tortilla and a gourd of water. These were the offerings the Hermit was accustomed to receiving from his pilgrim-visitors. . . .

Whose House Is This, Anyway?

It's not unusual for Joel Martin to talk about ghosts. After all, his radio show often dealt with such things. But still he was surprised when his friends the O'Neills asked for help with a real-life ghost story.

Martin joined psychic George Anderson for an actual on-the-air investigation. What they discovered was so startling that it provided them with a series of radio programs, a two-part show on cable television, and coverage by WABC-TV News, New York.

The O'Neills were desperate; they'd been tormented for a dozen years and could stand it no longer. Their house was a battleground—and the ghosts were winning the war!

> From ghoulies
> and ghosties
> and long-leggety beasties
> and things that go bump
> in the night—
> Good Lord deliver us!
>
> —Cornish prayer (a copy of which
>   hangs on a wall in the O'Neill
>   home)

Bill and Lynn O'Neill (not their real names), both in their late thirties, were comfortably middle-class, conservative people. They lived in a spacious white Colonial-style house on beautifully manicured grounds overlooking the water on Long Island's fashionable north shore. The house was built in the mid-nineteenth century in an area rich in Early American history; but neither Bill nor Lynn knew anything about the history of the house itself when they bought it.

The O'Neills could not understand why they had been so fortunate in purchasing the house at a price they described as a "steal." However, it did not take long after they moved in—the day after Halloween 1971—for the reason to become apparent. There was a problem almost from the moment they began living there.

The problem was ghosts.

It started while Lynn was redecorating. Portraits of the previous owners had been removed and were replaced with new photographs of the O'Neill family. But the new pictures did not stay on the walls for long—they were constantly falling off the picture hooks. Lynn thought that perhaps they were not hung properly, but no matter how she rehung them, the photographs would still end up on the floor.

Bill and Lynn would experience cold spots in various parts of the house that were otherwise warm. And then there were the closed doors that somehow opened . . . and the open doors that somehow shut. And the lights that turned off and on. At first Lynn and Bill thought they were having memory lapses or that Bill had turned on a light and Lynn had shut it off, forgetting to tell him.

Even when objects such as decorative plates started disappearing in the house, Bill thought Lynn was just being a good housekeeper, putting things neatly behind cupboard doors—until the objects could not be found anywhere!

One evening Bill was awakened from a nap by the sound of hobnailed boots in the hallway. Yet no one else was in the house. Gradually the unseen forces became more violent. Not only were the photographs torn from the walls, but books, pipes, canes, and other objects were thrown to the floor. The dining-room chandelier would mysteriously sway back and forth, its crystals tinkling furiously from the force.

Bill recalled one incident. "It sounded as if my cane collection was being thrown down and was rolling across the wooden floor. I thought it was a burglar. I went downstairs, but no one was there, and much to my surprise, the canes were not disturbed."

From time to time, the O'Neills heard the sound of a strumming guitar.

Once, Bill and Lynn were entertaining two friends in the sitting room when suddenly a book sailed out of the bookcase in the adjoining den and bounced off a wall. The four adults watched in disbelief.

The ghosts did not seem to respect or fear religious objects. In fact, it was just the opposite. Lynn had hung a crucifix on the wall of the master bedroom. Not only was the crucifix mysteriously ripped from the wall and thrown to the floor, but also the figure of Jesus Christ was broken off.

When the voices started, Bill and Lynn knew they were not alone in the house. Sometimes the playful, laughing voice of a child was heard, but the O'Neills had no children. A woman's voice could frequently be heard coming from an empty upstairs bedroom. And the O'Neills could stare directly at an empty staircase and hear the footsteps and the creaking boards of someone walking on the steps.

One night Lynn entered the master bedroom to get ready for bed—and stopped in her tracks. Sitting on the window seat was a stranger, a frail woman with blond hair, wearing a long turn-of-the-century dress. She was not transparent, as a Hollywood motion picture might portray a ghost, but solid. She stared past Lynn and did not give any indication that she saw her. When she stood up, she did not walk, but just drifted by mournfully. Moments later the apparition vanished as inexplicably as it had appeared.

Although the apparition and the various manifestations of the ghostly presence were unsettling, because they did not happen every day—and certainly not all at once—the O'Neills thought they could learn to live with a haunted house. And they certainly wouldn't *tell* anyone the house was haunted. On the other hand, they didn't have to.

An overnight guest, a woman visiting from another state, was so frightened that she left after spending only one night with the O'Neills. She swore she felt someone watching her. And a young woman tenant, who was renting a small cottage on the grounds, also claimed she was being watched.

But the terrifying sensation of being watched could not equal the real thing. The tenant finally fled in terror after she looked out the cottage window one afternoon and saw a stern old man staring back. He was dressed in a high-collared shirt and black coat. He had a sallow complexion, and smoked a pipe. He did not move and he didn't say a word. When she ran outside to confront him, no one was there. All she could find was a single set of footprints that led nowhere; the aroma of burning pipe tobacco still hung in the air.

The tenant never returned to the cottage after that. "You can think I'm crazy, but I think your house is haunted. I'm not staying here one more minute," she told Bill O'Neill.

Bill later learned that the tenant came from a family that had long lived in the area. In fact, her grandmother had resided in this same neighborhood years earlier. The young woman bore a strong physical resemblance to her grandmother when she was a young woman at the turn of the century. Did the ghostly presence at the window recognize something about the young woman which reminded him of her grandmother? Might the grandmother and the old man have known each other long ago? Or was there some other reason for the apparition?

Bill and Lynn continued to keep their secret, but they did notice one thing about the ghosts—they did not like women.

One day a young couple came to visit. The woman swore that some unseen force had pushed her, but the man with her never felt a thing. After that, the ghost turned its attention to Lynn. She was asleep one night when she was suddenly awakened by someone grabbing hold of her legs.

"Bill?" Lynn sleepily inquired.

The answer was a violent tugging on her ankles. It wasn't Bill; there was no one there that she could see, but Lynn fought back nonetheless. She held fast to the bed so she would not be pulled from it, all the while screaming and kicking furiously. The commotion woke Bill, who tried to help her, but whatever had hold of her did not let go.

Finally Lynn screamed: "Whatever you are, get away from me and leave me alone!"

To her surprise, it obeyed her and she was released. At that point, she fainted.

After that, the O'Neills had many sleepless nights; their nerves were constantly on edge. It was as if unseen forces were treating Bill and Lynn as intruders in their own house.

Should they move? They talked of it. Lynn was afraid that they were in physical danger and that if they remained in the house they were destined to have their peace persistently shattered. Eventually they would become emotionally drained; they were close to it now. Or could they even be driven insane by the actions of ghosts? Bill became increasingly disturbed by the activity. "If whatever it is can influence matter on our plane, what's the difference between throwing a book and picking up a knife?" he asked.

Could they somehow learn to live with the agitated and obviously unfriendly ghosts, or was there some way to force the spirits out?

"Why should we be the ones to leave the house?" Bill demanded. "We paid for it. We decorated it. We love it. I want to stay."

"If we can . . ." added Lynn.

The only precaution Bill could think of after the attack on Lynn was to secure a dead bolt to the bedroom door so they could lock it from the inside. Neither of them stopped to think that ghosts do not need invitations to enter rooms day or night. And spirit entities certainly are not discouraged or deterred by locked doors.

Whatever the phenomenon was, it had become increasingly frightening to them. They wondered not only what it was but also why it haunted their house.

Bill and Lynn could not tell anyone else: they would be called crazy. It remained their secret until, out of frustration, Bill told Joel Martin.

Martin is a well-known Long Island, New York, broadcaster with a large and loyal following for his programs about psychic phenomena. He is one of the nation's most experienced and knowledgeable talk-show hosts on that subject. He has interviewed, on radio and television, hundreds of well-known people and experts in many aspects of the paranormal. George Anderson appeared on his show hundreds of times, and later wrote *We Don't Die* with Joel.

Bill O'Neill knew Martin personally as well as professionally. One evening he called Martin to chance telling him about the problem with ghosts that he and Lynn were experiencing.

Joel Martin was more than happy to talk to an old friend, despite his busy schedule. He was hosting a nightly radio talk show that frequently centered around the occult; it was heard throughout Long Island and in parts of New York City and Connecticut on WBAB(FM). In addition, Joel hosted a weekly cable-television show for Viacom.

Joel and Bill chatted for a while before Bill could bring himself to the problem at hand. "It's about my house," he explained haltingly. "I think it's haunted."

This announcement startled Joel; he'd never heard the O'Neills mention anything about this the dozen years they lived in their house.

"Can you tell me about it?" Joel prompted.

"Well," Bill began, "it's—"

Suddenly Bill's words were obscured by a burst of static.

"What did you say?" Joel asked.

"—about the house—" Bill's voice could be heard in fits and starts. The crackling static made conversation impossible.

"—we'll have to come over and discuss this in person," Bill's voice finally came through. "How about next Thursday?"

"Fine," Joel agreed. "I'll speak to you then."

On Thursday, however, when Bill called to set up the appointment, the same thing happened. As long as the conversation was not about the house, there was no problem. When Bill began to talk about the haunting, the strange, unexplained static blotted out his words.

When Bill and Lynn made the long drive to see Joel, they asked if he could bring to the house one of the highly regarded psychics who appeared regularly on his radio and TV programs. Could such an individual, in strictest confidence, locate the source of the eerie disturbances?

Bill's request came as a surprise. He was not the kind to fabricate a story like this. In fact, he had never before publicly expressed any interest in psychic phenomena.

Joel Martin asked his old friend George Anderson if he would be willing to investigate a house that might be haunted. George was told nothing else about the house or the circumstances, since it is always best in such situations to let the psychic do the speaking. George agreed to try.

Anderson was thirty years old at the time, tall and slim and easygoing. His most prominent feature was his large piercing blue eyes. His wavy hair was neatly styled. George had a reputation for accuracy in his numerous appearances on radio and television and in public and private psychic readings.

George, Joel Martin, and several other people went to the house to both witness and document whatever might transpire there. Each of George's two visits was recorded first for radio, then for radio and television.

Once inside the house, George walked through the downstairs rooms—den, dining room, kitchen, and sitting room with large glass doors and many plants. He chose to stop first in the kitchen.

"Has anything ever been mysteriously taken from here?" he asked.

"Yes," Bill told him.

In the den George inquired if objects had been thrown around, moved, or in any other way inexplicably disturbed. Again he was told yes.

"Did you ever hear the sound of rustling of a woman's skirt? Because I feel the presence of a young woman from the late 1800's or the early 1900's," George explained.

Bill replied that he and Lynn were constantly finding sequins on the floor, those small reflective decorations worn on dresses. But, he hastened to clarify, they did not have any sequined materials in the house.

George listened attentively and nodded at each affirmation of his psychic impressions, but otherwise said little. He walked from room to room, followed quietly by Joel Martin and the others who accompanied him. He observed the details and furnishings of each room: poking, probing, banging, and tapping walls and ceilings.

"There are definitely different levels of energy, which vary from room to room. It feels like illness. I felt it in the dining room. There was the feeling of a draining presence in the den. That room had an energy level in it that could affect electrical items," George explained.

Next he went upstairs to the second floor, where he walked through several bedrooms. He went through two of them silently. But when he walked into a third bedroom, he stopped abruptly. This was Bill and Lynn's master bedroom.

The room was simply furnished. There was a window seat directly ahead as one entered the room. The window looked out on the landscaped grounds, toward the water, which was beyond the trees and gently rolling hills. To the left of the window was a large four-poster bed. On one of the posts hung a set of large wooden Catholic rosary beads with a cross, a present to Lynn. Over the bed hung a crucifix. To the right of the bed was a dresser holding a lamp and a small antique pitcher and basin. Near the bed on a night table was another, smaller lamp.

"This is the room where the heart of the problem is," George said. "This is the evil part of the house.

Sadness and tears of illness are in this room. I definitely feel there was a murder committed in or near the house."

George's announcement caught the group by surprise. Bill and Lynn looked visibly shaken.

George waited momentarily as psychic sights and sounds came to him. Then he explained that a woman had once sat in this room, ill, often at the window seat alone, many years ago. Here, he said, there had been an emotional conflict between her and a man. "Secrets were well-hidden in this house," George said. He described the man as middle-aged and very stern-looking, with gaunt features. He had steel-gray hair and beard, deep-set unyielding eyes, and a fixed expression. He had been very rigid in life and remained that way in spirit. His clothing looked like that from the turn of the century: dark coat and pants and stiff, high-collared shirt.

"He looks like he worked with his hands. All he ever knew was hard work—farming, physical labor. I'm getting the feeling this was his home. And he ruled it with an iron hand. He was very religious. Protestant. An old-fashioned fundamentalist in his thinking, devout in his beliefs, but rigid. And I don't think he liked Catholics. He's calling them 'papists,' the old term for Roman Catholics," George explained.

George had been staring in one direction, and now he turned toward the window.

"In the window seat a woman's spirit appears now. She's attractive but frail-looking. She's wearing a long dress of the kind worn eighty or more years ago. She says the spirit of the man who just appeared was that of her husband in life. They had a poor relationship, especially in the emotional sense. The husband had fixed ideas about what a wife should be, but his definition did not include words like 'love' and 'affection,' or the display of feelings. That is what caused their rift.

She was lonely and starved for love. He could not express it. They had a daughter. She appears to me now as a young woman in her teens. She's very high-spirited. In her life she was very unlike her father or mother.

"There is a third person about whom the man and his wife fought in their life together. It's a man younger than the husband was. He's a servant, like a handyman—a transient. The woman had an affair with him. She didn't do it to cheat on her husband. She did it because she yearned to be loved and the servant offered that.

"Her husband caught them, however, and the two men quarreled and then fought. The husband beat the servant to death in a fit of anger, but more out of a sense of honor than a desire to kill another human being. He killed him with a heavy blunt instrument such as a cane or farm tool. After all, he had found an adulterer with his wife. In the eyes of such a strict religious man of eighty or more years ago that was sin enough to justifiably enrage him. That's what he thought then. He later felt remorse for killing the servant, however.

"I feel the body of the murdered servant is still buried somewhere close by," George concluded chillingly.

But what did an account of a troubled family who lived in this house many years ago have to do with the disturbing behavior of ghosts in the present?

George explained that each psychic manifestation experienced by Bill and Lynn was, in fact, connected to the family who occupied this house long ago.

Then George stared at the rosary beads hanging on the bedpost. They began to move—swaying back and forth of their own volition. George also psychically knew that the crucifix had been ripped from the bedroom wall.

"His spirit regards any Catholic symbol in this house—which he still considers his home—as a sign of blasphemy. That angered him in life, and has carried on into his spirit existence.

"Other women in this house upset him too. It is a continuing resentment born of the fact that his wife had committed adultery. Even after all these years, his spirit cannot bear to release all its emotions about that.

"Their daughter was the kind to play tricks, make mischief. Her spirit is responsible for the disappearances of small objects and household items," George explained. Then he turned to the O'Neills.

"Has the entire family—husband, wife, and daughter—ever materialized so that you could see, hear, or feel their presences?"

Yes, they confirmed.

George returned downstairs to explain the cause of the books, canes, and pipes that had been strewn about the den floor. He said the old man's spirit was also responsible. Again, it was his way of expressing displeasure that someone else was living in *his* house.

Individual ghosts manifest for different reasons, George explained. Their behavior is not unlike that of people in the flesh. Ghosts can exhibit the same range of emotions. After all, their dimension, the afterlife, is parallel to our own, and they need to grow and develop just as we do, even though they are not on our own earthly plane. Ghosts are what we are going to be when we pass on.

This ghost did not realize that he was dead, in the sense that we use the word. As far as this spirit was concerned, Bill and Lynn were living in *his* house. He had long chased intruders from here. The problem now was that, unlike others, Bill and Lynn refused to leave.

George explained that this was a disturbed and confused spirit who felt he was still alive and could not accept the next dimension, or, as George calls it, "the other side." (George's and Joel's book, *We Don't Die*, makes this quite clear.)

Why did the ghost have difficulty making the transition from here to the hereafter?

"The other side seemed different from what he had been taught in his strict Protestant upbringing and he simply could not adjust to it. He had been expecting the joys of heaven or the horrors of hell, as they had been taught to him. He could not tolerate that the afterlife was not as he had envisioned it when he was on earth. So he summoned the energy to stay in this dimension of the living, although he no longer belonged here. He has remained earthbound all these years since his 'death.' In doing so he has intimidated his dutiful wife and daughter to also remain earthbound. They agreed out of a sense of old-fashioned obedience to stay in what they considered to be familiar surroundings. None of these spirits think of themselves as dead. To them, time has stopped as we would know it," George explained.

He added, "The old man's ghost continues to haunt anything or anybody with whom he disagreed in life. That would include Roman Catholics, anyone else living in 'his' house, strangers who might visit, and especially women. He still has unresolved conflicts and has not learned to forgive and forget."

George went outside to the small cottage near the main house. He said this was where the wife and servant had had their love affair and where they were caught by her husband. After the wife's infidelity was discovered, she returned to the house, where she remained alone—often at the window seat of her bedroom—until she died of consumption several years later, George said.

He went on to explain that any woman in the cottage was certain to feel the troubled presence of the old man's ghost. He was correct, of course, because it was from here that the woman tenant had fled in terror after seeing the spirit materialize at the cottage window.

George went next to a garage that had been converted from an old carriage house. He was accompanied by Joel Martin, Bill, Lynn, and the observer group as he walked up an outside staircase to the second floor. The ground floor was locked. It was evening, dark outside now, and George's immediate impression of the carriage house was that it was "eerie." It was a description no one disagreed with.

George said he experienced pain in his head, and nausea. "I get the feeling I'm being watched. Once I walked in here, I felt overpowered," he said. "This is where the husband and the servant argued. The servant lived here. He was a bad-tempered character. There was a violent fight about the wife who had committed adultery, and the old man struck a killing blow to the servant's head and upper back and bludgeoned the man to death—"

Just then, as George spoke, the group heard a loud booming sound coming from underneath—the locked first floor of the carriage house. No person present on the second floor could have been responsible for the thudding.

"What was that?" George exclaimed.

"I don't know," Joel Martin answered.

"Did you feel that?" Bill asked.

"I felt it, and it was underneath us," George answered.

Joel agreed. "Right under our feet."

"But there's no way anyone could get in down there," Bill said.

George and the group froze momentarily with fear, and then quickly left the building.

Was a spirit interrupting? Had the old man's unsettled ghost once more made its presence known by expressing displeasure that it was being talked about? Did he feel that this group of people was prying into his life?

The incident reminded Joel Martin of the time he and Bill had spoken on the telephone several weeks earlier. Each time they turned to the subject of the haunted house, there was static that made the phone call inaudible. Could the disquieted spirit have caused interference again, to prevent a conversation about him?

George was asked if he could do anything to restore peace to the house. Did he have the power to send the ghosts back to the next dimension where they belonged but refused to go?

George returned to the bedroom of the main house, where he felt the conflict between the husband and wife had originally been centered. George had brought with him a crucifix and picture of St. Michael the Archangel, which he placed on the bed. Then he said a prayer for the spirits who had been haunting the house. He exhorted the confused and disturbed souls to return to the next dimension and cross into the light.

St. Michael the Archangel is a very powerful saint who fights evil and negative souls and helps by saving them. Thus George hoped that strong prayers, and his insistence to the spirits that they go where they belonged, would force the ghosts from the house and correct the situation. He said that with troubled souls it was necessary to speak directly and sternly.

However, until George stepped in with his psychic expertise and the religious symbols combined with prayer, the spirits of the three family members who had once occupied the house had been unable to progress to the other side because of their unresolved conflicts. They needed assistance and guidance to make the transition.

Thus George had told them to pass over, had summoned the help of a powerful saint, and had prayed for them. George also asked where the murdered servant was buried.

A disembodied voice, which only he could hear, guided him to the basement of the house. There he found a false wall on one side of the dimly lit, damp, low-ceilinged cellar. He bravely walked behind the wall to a small room where a mysterious mound of earth resembling a grave was located.

Was this the grave of the murdered servant? Bill admitted that since he and Lynn had moved in and, much to their shock, first found the cryptlike room in the basement twelve years earlier, they had always been suspicious of it. However, they could never summon the courage to dig there. So they had simply left the "grave" just as they found it.

The small group went upstairs. Bill and Lynn were still concerned. Was there reason to fear the spirit entities? George explained that in his experience, most ghosts were "misunderstood." They were not all necessarily evil, although they could be troublesome, annoying, and even frightening. He said they were psychologically disturbed in a sense because they were refusing to progress.

He added, "I've never heard of such a thing, but I can't say an act of violence wouldn't or couldn't be committed by such a spirit."

Neither Bill nor Lynn had knowingly caused the problem. And they were luckier than many others: thanks to a gifted psychic-medium, their nerve-racking years appeared to be over. It had taken a combination of stern words and the power of prayer to move the ghosts from the house they had lived in long ago, to the next dimension, where they now belonged, so that their souls might progress. George had helped to guide them into the light of the other side and—hopefully—to adjust and eventually find peace.

After the O'Neills' twelve years of coexistence in the same house with a family of disturbed souls—by which time they were emotionally drained and often terrified—a psychic had explained the problem to *both* families.

George had solved the mystery of what had been discovered to be an intolerant, confused ghost and his family.

Will the spirits ever return? No one can say for certain. Bill and Lynn were, of course, grateful to George. Since his last visit the house has been quiet. But the O'Neills never have summoned the nerve to dig up the strange mound of earth in their basement. There is a new tenant in the cottage. A man. He has not reported any problems with ghosts. Occasionally Bill and Lynn think they hear a strange noise, but nothing has ever disappeared again, although the household objects taken by one of the ghosts to another dimension, or hidden, have never been returned. No more objects have been thrown around. No spirit apparitions have appeared to either of them or to any visitors—male or female.

Many times, Bill and Lynn have invited George to spend the night with them in the house. George has so far politely declined the invitation.

Meanwhile, the dead bolt remains on the inside of the bedroom door—just in case. Who knows? Perhaps the ghosts might get homesick and return someday. They may be wondering, even now: Whose house is this, anyway?

The Man with Healing Hands

---

*Pearl Gonzalez is an American journalist with a
longtime interest in the paranormal. She has traveled throughout the United States and Mexico, as
well as to Europe, interviewing many prominent
people in the field. But the most extraordinary person she's ever met is Bill Clark, a psychic healer
who has escaped death innumerable times. His story
is incredible, yet thousands can attest to the healing
touch of his hands, including Pearl Gonzalez herself.
With the exception of Pearl, Bill, and Rosemarie
Clark, all the names have been changed.*

Bill Clark is an unassuming man. He dresses simply, is
slim but muscular, and stands five feet, eight inches,
weighing about 140 pounds. His bright eyes shine out
through layers of wrinkles that spread upward from an
easygoing grin. Once in a while he enjoys a beer. He used
to enjoy fishing, but now there's no time for that.

It is surprising that Bill Clark managed to survive for
all of his nearly eighty years. He made his living as a
laborer in a variety of jobs, and his was most certainly a
roller-coaster life, as he barely survived numerous near-
fatal accidents. Some accidents did terrible damage to his
body and others he miraculously emerged from unscathed.

Bill always thought his injuries were the will of God, but their real reason would eventually become apparent.

It all began in 1921, when Bill was a fourth-grade student living in the Bronx, New York. After school, he worked for a local tailor. One afternoon, he had just finished delivering a suit in a large building when he decided to forgo the elevator and walk down the stairs instead. On the way down he stopped to look out the ninth-floor window at the café below. His quarter tip fell out of his shirt pocket. Bill lunged for it and suddenly he found himself on the ground, resting on top of a hedge with nothing more serious than an arm scraped from wrist to elbow. He told his mother he had tripped on the sidewalk.

A year later he was in a sleighing accident and hit the back of his head on solid ice. He was examined by a doctor, who marveled at the close call. Had the crack in Bill's skull touched a main artery, he would have died. However, Bill missed three months of school while the concussion healed.

Bill managed to reach the age of sixteen, and in 1927 he was working for the Diamond Match Company. One morning, he raced to catch an express train. He dropped his nickel in the turnstile and ran across the subway platform, but he missed the train. A few minutes later, he heard a horrible rumbling sound. He looked down the tunnel, in the direction of the train, and saw smoke. There had been a terrible collision and 123 people were killed or injured. Bill chalked up this near-miss to luck.

In 1943 Bill worked as a laborer at Stewart Field, Newburgh, New York. One day he was walking through the largest airplane hangar on the field. He didn't know why, but he had the sudden urge to look up. It saved his life.

Three ten-foot-long beams had come loose and

were crashing down on him. The first beam split his chin. The second hit his shoulder. The third his thigh. Bill fell to the floor, bleeding heavily. When the airport nurse arrived, she was shocked by the intense bleeding and covered him with a blanket while she waited for the ambulance that would quickly whisk him to the nearby dispensary. There doctors discovered the split chin looked much worse than it was. Though it took a long time for his chin to heal, it was the only serious damage. But if Bill hadn't looked up, the beam would have crushed his skull.

Two years later, in 1945, Bill was flying through Alameda, California, in a small five-seater plane when the aircraft crashed. He was the only survivor.

Not long after this, Bill moved back to New York, taking his growing family with him. They moved to his hometown, Highland Mills, where he worked for the railroad as a brakeman. He was working on a stopped passenger train in a station when a sudden jerking motion sent him flying down between the cars and onto the track. Stunned senseless, he couldn't move. But the conductor spotted Bill just before he was about to pull out. He and another conductor dragged him out from under the wheels of the train. Bill had suffered another concussion.

In 1950, while still in Highland Mills, he was working at a private residence as a caretaker. The house's roof needed repairs and, being conscientious, Bill climbed up to do the work. He promptly fell off the roof, landed on his head and suffered from amnesia for nine days.

Later that same year, Bill was working for the Convent of Jesus and Mary. He was clearing away foliage from around the building when he felt a tap and a sting on his wrist. He saw a single mark on his arm, assumed it had been a bee hidden in the flowers and leaves, and shrugged it off. But soon afterward he fell gravely ill for six weeks and didn't care if he lived or died.

It wasn't a bee that had stung Bill. He'd been bitten on the wrist by a copperhead snake. One of its fangs had struck his watchband, while the other had pierced his flesh.

In 1961 Bill was reading water meters for the City of Miami Beach when a truck drove into him and broke his arm. A few years later, on a family boating trip, a huge wave lifted the boat up out of the water and dropped it down with a violent motion. Bill's back was broken. Eventually he went back to work, wearing a brace; but after several weeks, he removed it himself. The doctors couldn't understand how he managed, but he was functioning without pain and without the brace, so they let it stay off. Bill's back hasn't bothered him since.

Just when Bill's friends and relatives thought the list of bizarre accidents could not get any longer, the most significant event of all—the one that changed his life—occurred in Florida on June 6, 1968.

That rainy afternoon, Bill was inspecting cars for the North Miami Beach Police Department. Around 3:15 P.M., lightning came through an open door, struck Bill on his hand, lifted and threw him into a far wall, and passed through his body a second time. The building was plunged into darkness. Horrified coworkers ran to his side—but Bill stood up, miraculously uninjured. Their horror turned to amazement. They saw—and later testified to the fact—that there were no burns or other marks on him, and Bill went on working for the rest of the afternoon.

All of those who witnessed the incident said it was a bolt of lightning that struck Bill. But Bill reported, "It was large and round, larger than a basketball. And it came straight at me. It was a ball of lightning."

Shortly after this, Bill would rethink the lightning theory, and the reason for the long list of his accidents would finally become known.

A few weeks later, Bill rose and dressed for work, and went into the kitchen. It had begun as an ordinary morning until he found his wife, Marion sitting at the breakfast table, shaking.

Marion told Bill he had been talking in his sleep ever since the accident. But he wasn't talking in English. And now he had done more than talk in a strange language:

"Last night," she said, "you sat up in bed, turned to let your feet touch the floor, and slowly crossed your hands on your chest. When you turned your head toward me, your eyes opened and you had a strange expression on your face."

Marion told a stunned Bill that as he had looked at her, he spoke in archaic English and in a female voice: "Fear me not: I come in peace. Your mate has the power to heal. Make him use it."

Bill laughed; his wife obviously had had a nightmare. But soon after, he began having odd dreams, his body went numb, and he'd experience automatic writing. He thought he was losing his mind. He had had strange visions of a beautiful woman, in ancient Egyptian garb. She would appear to him in his dreams and ask if he remembered his princess. He would then find himself standing in an ancient courtyard, with people dressed in an ancient way. They would greet him as a prince and talk in a "funny" language, which he didn't recognize but which he understood.

The woman, Princess Tara, told him they are soulmates and lived a past life together in 731 B.C. She took him on astral journeys, including being inside the Sphinx and the Great Pyramid. The princess remarked that most people didn't realize the two great structures were connected, that sand over the centuries had covered the lower buildings.

The princess described a "land of the rising sun" as their homeland. Did she mean Japan?

The princess also told Bill that all the accidents he had survived were a result of her lengthy attempts to reach him. Since it took a severe accident to bring him to the level of consciousness where the princess could contact him, she, the princess had been orchestrating the accidents—but she had also been guiding and protecting him at the same time.

It was not easy for Bill's wife and family to deal with this new turn of events. They didn't know what to make of it and they weren't sure how much their boarder, Ellen Wortman, had heard. But Bill's daughter tried to solve the mystery. When he described the dreams to her, she and a friend tried to locate information about the Egyptian princess and the land of the rising sun. They went through all sorts of books in the public libraries, but without results.

Then one afternoon Bill and his daughter were alone in the house when Bill went into a trance . . . and the princess began to speak through Bill. His daughter did not panic. Instead, she asked the princess where her father had come from. She placed her hand, holding a pencil, on a map. Her hand moved across the map in different directions while the princess nodded either yes or no. Finally she said, "Stop." When it came to rest, the pencil was pointing to present-day Iraq.

As if the presence of the mysterious princess wasn't enough, another unusual thing began to happen to Bill. After the lightning struck, he found that his body was slowly becoming numb. The numbness had started in the feet and was slowly working its way upward. Once during this phase, Bill cut his leg with a saw and didn't know it because he didn't feel it. It wasn't until he saw blood dripping down his leg that he realized what had happened.

Bill became very knowledgeable on subjects he had had no previous knowledge of. Through the princess's guidance he found he could converse with archaeologists, scientists, and doctors. The words would just come out. These professionals often asked Bill how he knew about such things. His only clue was that it all began when the lightning struck.

Once, the Clarks' boarder, Ellen Wortman came home one evening gasping for breath. Ellen, who suffered from angina pectoris, could hardly take more than five steps without taking pills for her heart condition.

Although Marion had mixed feelings, she remembered the princess's admonition. "This is an excellent opportunity for you to start healing!"

Bill was reluctant. He thought he'd make a fool of himself. But Ellen kept gasping for air and pointed to her chest to show where the pain was. Suddenly, Bill felt totally in command.

"Turn around," he told Ellen. He felt he had to work from behind her.

He reached out and touched her back. Immediately he lost his breath and was gasping for air. He felt terribly sick and suffered for four days afterward—but the next day Ellen awoke feeling fine. Two days later she stopped drinking, smoking, and taking her pills. She soon went from 84 to 106 pounds.

It took four days for Bill's pain to wear off. He realized that because the numbness hadn't yet reached his hands, his first healing had proved to be very painful. When the numbing of his body gradually completed itself, subsequent healings had no effect on him.

Healing Ellen was only the beginning. As word got around, Bill was asked to help numerous afflicted people, many of whom later reported either vast improvement or total healing. Eventually his files bulged with thank-you notes and documented testimonials from nearly fifty thousand people—copies of which are available to the public. And these files include only the people who have reported back!

In the search for answers to what happened to him, Bill went back to the doctors who had examined him after he was struck by lightning. He saw Dr. Ronald K. Wright, former chief medical examiner of Dade County, Dr. Stanly Dean of Miami, and Dr. Uwe Giertz of Fort Lauderdale. They could do nothing more than validate his abilities.

In the mid 1970's Bill was also tested by the privately run Mankind Research Foundation in Washington, D.C. One of its scientists, J. K. Paul Sauvin, measured Bill's electrodynamic field using Burr's field-measurement technique. Informal findings indicated that voltage variation occurred simultaneously between healer and the subject being healed. More simply stated, when Bill is healing, he is recharging the human battery.

When Sauvin photographed Bill's fingertips with a Kirlian camera, photographs revealed a large boost of energy while Bill was in the process of healing. Sauvin said the field-pattern characteristics were totally unlike anything ever seen before, and warranted further research.

One of Bill's most outstanding cases involved a boy who had been born with a hole in his heart. In 1971 Jonathan was eleven years old; he lived in Miami Lakes, Florida. He was scheduled for open-heart surgery, but his mother, Grace, wanted to avoid an operation. She asked Bill to work on her son.

Bill visited Jonathan's home that Wednesday—and every Wednesday evening—for six weeks. During the first visit, he listened to the boy's chest and heard a beat and a suction sound. The sound alarmed him.

Every time he visited Jonathan, he heard the same thing.

Then Jonathan's mother postponed Bill's next visit. It was Jonathan's birthday—he was twelve years old and she was throwing a small party for him.

On the seventh week, Bill returned and again listened to Jonathan's chest. This time all he heard was a normal thumping. The suction sound was gone. Jonathan's mother told Bill she somehow knew the hole had closed. When she brought her son to the doctor, the amazed heart specialist said the hole had become undetectable and no surgery was necessary. He couldn't explain it.

When he was fourteen years old, Jonathan won the Presidential Award for Physical Fitness. As a younger boy he could never participate in sports. Bill did not see Jonathan again until he was twenty-seven years old, and found him to be in excellent physical condition.

In January 1972 Mr. and Mrs. George Peters of Miami called on Bill. George had leukemia and he was on his way to the doctor for a checkup, but his wife insisted she wanted Bill's touch first. Bill would see George every time he was due for a checkup, and then George would proceed to the doctor's office. The doctor couldn't understand why his patient was showing such marked improvement. Finally the bewildered doctor pronounced him cured.

Several years later, George Peters had a relapse. Bill healed him again. Mrs. Peters told Bill he was driving the doctors crazy. They kept asking her if she was doing anything different, but on Bill's advice she never told them. By now her husband had declared he would never go near a doctor again. He felt that as long as Bill was around, he'd be all right.

Unfortunately, the years went by and Bill moved away and lost touch with the Peters. One night, nine years later, Bill thought of Mr. Peters and called his home. Mrs. Peters said her husband had recently contracted pneumonia. Since their attempts to locate Bill had failed—Bill had been living out of state for a few years—George had died.

Animals have also benefited from Bill's gifted hands. One evening in November 1971 Bill received a phone call from a young girl named Evelyn. She was baby-sitting a German shepherd named Leo, owned by a Mr. and Mrs. Buddy Lewis of North Miami. Evelyn apologized for asking Bill to work on an animal, but her affection for Leo overcame her hesitancy.

Leo had recently been hit by a car: his back, pelvis, and one rear leg were broken. A veterinarian had treated Leo, but recommended putting him out of his misery. He claimed it would take six months for Leo to get well, and even at that, Leo would never walk again. The Lewises were very upset over this prognosis.

When Bill entered the Lewis home, Evelyn ushered him to a room where he found Leo lying on a blanket. At first he feared the dog might attack him, but Leo couldn't even move. Bill laid his hand on the dog's head. Nothing happened; the dog didn't move. But when Bill touched the animal's spine, Leo raised his head and started to lick Bill's hand.

Evelyn left the room while Bill worked with Leo, who lay motionless once again on the blanket. Bill walked over to a sofa and sat down.

"Here, Leo. Come on, boy," Bill called.

Leo jumped up and walked over to Bill. Again he licked Bill's hand. Bill led the dog over to his untouched bowls of food and water. Leo had been unable to move or eat by himself. Now he ate heartily before returning to lie on the blanket.

When Evelyn returned, it appeared as though Leo hadn't moved from where he lay on the blanket. "What are Leo's chances?" she asked worriedly.

Bill told her to call Leo. Bewildered, Evelyn did as she was told. Leo rose and walked to her.

Evelyn let out a shriek—Bill says to this day he can still hear her screams of joy. Later that evening Mrs. Lewis came home, hardly able to believe the change in her pet.

Once Bill healed Sam, his daughter's cat. In 1974, while Bill was visiting his daughter in Tallahassee, Florida, Sam disappeared. A neighbor found him, but Sam was in terrible shape; he'd been mauled by a dog. The neighbor brought Sam to a veterinarian who wouldn't operate for fear the cat would die.

They took Sam home, where Bill worked on the cat's wounds for several days. Fifteen years later, Sam is still alive. . . .

Bill now feels that animals respond faster than humans. Although he's been able to effect instant healing on humans, it's more likely to happen with animals. He doesn't know why.

Bill's new life of healing underwent further changes. As the years went by, his wife became very jealous of the princess, who continued to make her presence known. Bill found it odd that Marion was jealous of someone who had been dead over a thousand years. But perhaps because of the pressure and constant demands of Bill's life-style, Marion begged him to give up healing. But this was unthinkable to Bill, and so he refused. After thirty-nine years of marriage, seven children, twenty grandchildren, and nine great-grandchildren, Bill and Marion divorced.

Needing a change of scenery, Bill drove up to the Washington, D.C., area, staying at the home of some old friends, Donald and Lorraine Reed of Reston, Virginia. The Reeds were interested in furthering Bill's work, so they set up a healing group. Bill continued with his work in the D.C. area for a while, assisted by Rita Mae Thomas, whom he subsequently married.

During this period in the mid-seventies, healing sessions would be held three or four times a week, sometimes at the Reeds', other times at the home of a free-lance writer. Bill would work on eighteen to twenty-four people a night. He enjoyed these sessions. "They were almost like a party," he said of their festive atmosphere.

One of the "guests" who benefited from Bill's healing touch was Violet Clifton, who lived in Reston. She had a bladder and kidney infection and later caught pneumonia. Despite medical treatment, she was slowly fading away. After just three treatments by Bill, she recovered.

One night, while Bill was working on someone, there was a sudden commotion at the front door. Three people entered, carrying a very sick man, Charles Dorheimer from Pittsburgh.

Immediately Bill sat him on a chair and loosened the man's clothing, putting his hands on Dorheimer's bare chest. As he did so, he heard a woman gasp—as blood ran from his arms down to the floor.

One of the most peculiar aspects of Bill's healing was his bleeding arms. (This phenomenon was captured on film by Channel 4's local news in Washington, D.C., and televised in November 1974.) Sometimes blood can be seen welling up under his skin as he works. His arms are covered with white scars from previous healings. Bill explained that the bleeding worked as a pressure valve when the energy being transmitted to the patient became too intense. Rita Mae usually wiped the blood away with a disinfectant so Bill could continue uninterrupted.

Four days later, Charles Dorheimer, who had been frightened away by Bill's bleeding during his first session, was back. This time he walked in by himself. Bill started to put his hands on him, then stopped.

"What's wrong?" Dorheimer asked. "Why don't you continue?"

"My help is no longer needed," Bill replied.

Bill's procedure—for all except heart patients—was to place his hands on a person's back. His hands would then begin to shake rhythmically, giving one the feeling of being hooked up to an electric vibrator. Occasionally he would dramatically fling his hands to the side as if shaking off something unwanted. If the patient had an illness, Bill's arms would make a crackling sound, almost like a Geiger counter finding its target.

Unlike the "drawing out" of illness from heart patients, Bill described his technique as "welding [the heart] together." He would place his hands on both the front and back of a person, and both his hands would then vibrate.

When Bill finished treating a patient, he would draw several crosses near the spot undergoing treatment. He admitted that while healing, he always sees another pair of smaller hands placed over his. As to whose they can be, "Who was the greatest healer?" Bill has always replied.

Bill and Rita Mae moved back to Florida to be close to his family. But after a year they returned to Reston. One night, a woman approached Bill. She hugged him and said she was Mrs. Dorheimer. When she had heard Bill was back, she flew in from Pittsburgh to thank him. She hadn't told anyone, when her husband had been carried in the year before, that he was dying from cancer and had three weeks to live. Now all signs of cancer had disappeared and he was back to his normal weight and his old job.

After several years in Reston, Bill and Rita Mae went back to Florida. They made West Palm Beach their headquarters, as Bill continued healing and lecturing. He traveled to forty-one states and four other countries: Colombia, Mexico, Haiti, and Canada. As word of his healing spread, he appeared on numerous radio and television shows. Newspaper and magazine articles abound and have appeared throughout the United States, in foreign countries he visited—and even in ones he didn't visit, such as England and Japan.

Bill even lectured at Georgetown Medical School in Washington, D.C., in 1975. He lectured at colleges, high schools, and private and church groups around the country. His program includes his life story, a question-and-answer period, and invariably, healing sessions.

Often, during these public lectures, Princess Tara delighted in taking over Bill's body. She often appeared while Bill was healing, at large conferences, where she could address individuals and impart advice, Bill would find himself channeling for her. He always hated the feeling of her "coming in" and would try to fight her off. As she entered his body, the princess would rip off his shirt buttons or tear his shirt down the middle.

Before he could control it, however, Bill would be in a deep trance and the princess would take over.

The princess made her presence known as recently as the Seventh International Conference on Psychotronic Research, which was held December 2–5, 1988, at West Georgia College, Carrollton, Georgia.

Princess Tara would often say, "I didn't come to earth to condemn any mortal, but mankind must mend its ways." She insisted that the world and especially the United States had to resolve its racial strife. She absolutely refused to make any predictions about the future. The princess says she does not predict future events but only speaks the truth.

Sometimes she talked about past events. She did say that the Kennedy assassination was the result of President John F. Kennedy stepping on the toes of a man who was highly placed in world government. She talked about the political leaders of the country, especially Richard Nixon, just before Watergate.

Along with her admonitions about better human behavior, the princess delivered eloquent poetry describing events in her and Bill's lives.

Bill was called everything from a faith healer to a miracle worker to a psychic. But Bill preferred to think of himself as a man with helping hands.

Unfortunately, his increasing popularity affected his personal life once more. After seven years of marriage, Rita Mae divorced Bill after she announced she could no longer handle the nonstop activity. There seemed to be no time to rest, and no way to say no to the demands of those in need of healing.

Ten years ago Bill met and married a sensitive, spiritual woman in West Palm Beach. Rosemarie is also a healer. She is not as powerful as Bill, but is slowly growing in strength. He discovered her gift when they were first married and she instantly healed a muscle pull in his leg. Now, when Bill works on patients, her hands are on his shoulders. His power is stronger with Rosemarie and his healing more effective and longer-lasting. With her help, he has increased the number of people he can touch in an evening; he can handle up to thirty cases in one session.

After he is gone, Bill has said that Rosemarie will have enough energy to take over on her own. The princess has also informed them that Rosemarie must continue Bill's work.

In 1978 Bill attended the Congress on Paranormal Phenomena in Mexico City. There he met Pearl Gonzalez, who interviewed him for the magazine *Super Mente* (Super Mind). Bill described the accident that had changed his life and everything that had happened afterward.

Bill also told her that he was not about to perform psychokinetic tricks to prove his ability. He felt it would detract from his healing powers.

While he talked, Pearl felt an intense vibration just sitting near him. It was as though he was plugged into the elements.

Pearl was curious about his description of a numbness over his entire body. In an effort to prove this particular condition, Bill instructed Pearl to try sticking him with something, anything at all. Pearl picked up a fork and lightly touched him on the arm.

Bill laughed. "Don't be afraid. Try harder."

Urged on, Pearl pushed the fork deep into his flesh, almost drawing blood. Bill said he felt nothing.

Pearl told Bill she had painful arthritis in her wrists.

"There's a healing session this evening. Why don't you come?"

Of course, Pearl agreed. Whether or not anything happened, she could still write about it for the magazine. She went to the "healing room," a room set aside in the Hotel María Isabel, where the congress was being held. It was filled with folding chairs and looked like an ordinary conference room, only the people seated were waiting their turn for Bill Clark's miraculous touch. Pearl felt very confident. She had interviewed many healers before she met Bill, but none had ever measured up to the intensity of his vibrations.

When it was Pearl's turn, she noted that his hands hardly touched her flesh as they probed. When his hands touched her wrists, she heard a crackling noise. She heard the crackling sounds again, to a lesser degree, when his hands came near her stomach. She hadn't told Bill about her intestinal problem because she felt it was only a mild, temporary upset. But with Bill it wasn't necessary to give details; his hands did the diagnosing.

After he performed what Mexicans call a "cleansing," he shook out his hands as previously described. Then he signed crosses on her wrists.

Pearl laughed and said, "Hey, I'm a nice Jewish girl."

Bill grinned. "I treat everyone this way—Jews, Christians, Muslims, everybody."

Pearl's upset stomach miraculously cleared up immediately. The arthritis took a little longer. It came and went for about two months before it finally disappeared. That was over ten years ago.

During these healing sessions, Bill seemed more like a robot than a person. He'd be worn out when they were over. He immediately needed a glass of water, and took almost an hour to return to normal.

Since he expended a great deal of energy on healing, he does not want it wasted. When someone tries to "test" Bill, perhaps it is the princess who protects him. For example, during the filming of a television program, a crew member asked for a demonstration. When it came his turn to sit in the chair, Bill merely touched him. The man immediately shot off the chair as though hit by lightning. A second touch and he lay on the floor with his eyes rolled back in his head and appeared to be dead. It took about ten minutes for him to fully recover.

"That's what happens when someone takes up valuable time," Bill remarked.

People who cannot travel to see Bill personally can also be treated. All they have to do is send a full-length photo of themselves to him and they can receive long-distance healing. Some people have reported great success, while others saw no change at all.

Bill told Pearl that although he finds much gratification in being able to heal, he never ceases to question why this has happened to him. Why is it, he wonders, that a man like him, with an eighth-grade education, who all of his life worked as a laborer, caretaker, or carpenter, was chosen?

"There are so many people who gave up their whole lives—nuns, priests, missionaries. Why not somebody like them? They say the Creator works in strange ways. I would say this is one of his strange ways. I never stop wondering: why me?"

Bill accepts no payment for his work, and he and Rosemarie live mainly on his social-security check. Traveling expenses are paid either by a non-profit organization or by the individual who might request special services.

Once a Florida lawyer told Bill that with his powers, he was "sitting on a million dollars." The lawyer offered his "help," but Bill refused. He believes that if he turns commercial he might lose his power. Besides, Princess Tara told Bill that love of money is the whole reason for suffering on this earth. And Bill agrees with her.

After more than twenty years of healing, Bill finally accepted these many "miracles." At first he had been very excited about the healings. But by now he had seen people get up from wheelchairs and walk, move their paralyzed limbs, and recover from fatal illnesses. He handled almost every disease, disorder, and injury imaginable. He was no longer surprised when an accident victim got up and walked away at his touch; in fact, he thought nothing of his powers, except that he hoped everyone could recover. His explanation for his attitude was, "I know I'm not doing it. It's from somebody much higher."

But he *was* amazed by one astonishing event:

When his first wife left him, saying among other things that he was not the same man she had married, he knew he had changed—but not to what extent. A friend brought to his attention the fact that there was something different about his eyes.

Indeed there was something different. Over the years, his eyes, once brown, had turned blue, unmistakably blue—the color of electricity. . . .

The Peterson Poltergeist

Are all old houses haunted?

The Andrews family, who coveted the Peterson mansion for years, never considered the possibility . . . until it looked as though the late owner of their new home had never left. . . .

All the names have been changed, but the horror remains. . . .

The Andrews family was moving. After eight years of scrimping and saving, the Toronto family had finally purchased their dream house, and now they were carting their possessions down the stairs of their old home at East Toronto Street.

It was a very short move—only a couple of blocks away, to East Meadows—and the May weather that Tuesday morning in 1964 was beautiful, so the Andrews family hadn't bothered to hire a van. Instead, a caravan of friends and neighbors helped them carry furniture and crates down the sidewalk. The grand piano made the trip in the back of a half-ton truck, with one witty fellow playing tunes all the way.

The happy procession snaked back and forth between the old house and the new one. Actually, it wasn't a "new" house, it was a huge stone house over one hundred years old, and it looked haunted. A huge three-story structure of ornamental gray stone, it sprawled magnificently in the center of an overgrown grove of Chinese elm.

With its twin L-shaped verandas (one ground-level, one second-story), Doric columns, and corner turret, it was completely out-of-place among its prim row-house neighbors. The front door, located at the far end of the lower veranda, was painted dead black and had a bronze lion's-head knocker. The entire grounds were unkempt; for reasons unknown, the previous owners had neglected their yard work, and the lawn resembled a jungle.

The heat and the work soon put a damper on the party. By midafternoon the exhausted movers stopped to rest. Inside the new house, seventeen-year-old Lee, the oldest Andrews daughter, slumped with four tired neighbors at the kitchen table while her mother, Eva, brewed tea. They were just sipping their first cups when the afternoon calm was shattered by the crash of breaking glass.

There were, very clearly, two components to the sound: first the crash, then the tinkle of falling shards. Irritated and startled, Lee raced into the living room. She was certain that someone had broken a window. *Some kid with a baseball,* she thought, glancing at the windows. But all the panes were intact.

Her mother checked the bathroom: same result—nothing broken. One of the neighbors thought the noise had come from upstairs and went to look. Not a thing. Puzzled now, the moving party split up to investigate.

In the ten minutes that followed, the entire house—all three floors and eleven rooms—was searched from top to bottom. No broken glass was anywhere to be found. No windows had shattered, yet five people had distinctly heard the sound.

Lee was hardly surprised. She had suspected all her life that the old house was haunted. She and her childhood playmates had called the house on East Meadows "the witch's house." In fact, it had belonged to a respectable middle-aged couple, the Petersons, but they seldom went outside; it wasn't hard for the children to imagine that a witch really lived inside.

But the "witch" was not the youngsters' invention. Their parents had heard the same story, though none of them could say for certain where it had originated. It was a neighborhood legend.

The children had a favorite game; they would dare one another to run past the big mock-orange tree and peek in the lower windows of the old gray stone house. Ultimately, Lee's turn had come. Heart pounding, she had sprinted through the overgrown shrubbery, caught the edge of the sill, and, straining on tiptoes, looked in the lower turret window. A horribly fanged jet-black face glared back at her! With a shriek she let go, cleared the hedge in one leap, and raced down the street screaming, hotly pursued by her playmates. Only much later did she learn that she had not seen a demon. Mr. Peterson was a sailor and often brought home souvenirs from his voyages. The black face was only a ceremonial mask.

Lee's mother, Eva, had dreamed for years of owning the Peterson mansion, ever since she, her husband, Michael, a plumber, and their three children had lived in the neighborhood. Eva and Michael both worked and saved so they could move out of the old house on East Toronto Street, which they were rapidly outgrowing.

Until 1964 it had appeared that Eva's dream would go unfulfilled. Then tragedy intervened. Mr. Peterson, flying out of Toronto on a routine commercial flight, was killed when his plane crashed a few minutes after takeoff. The next week his widow put their house up for sale. Eva Andrews instantly made an offer. The bid was ridiculously low—about two-thirds the actual value of the house—but the bereaved Mrs. Peterson snapped it up. Eva had noticed that Mrs. Peterson seemed nervous, as if she were afraid to stay alone, but Eva thought it was because of her husband's sudden death. Within two days Mrs. Peterson was gone, leaving most of her late husband's belongings behind.

And so the Andrews family moved in—to be welcomed by the sound of breaking glass. That would prove to be the least of their strange troubles.

The structure itself seemed connected with the number thirteen. Its street number added up to it, and the eleven-room mansion actually had two extra rooms, which brought the total to thirteen. One room was discovered in the basement, behind the stairs; the other, in the turret attic. The basement room contained nothing of importance: the remains of a small wooden box, some broken necklaces, and a few coins. It was accessible only through a passageway too narrow for an adult, so the Andrewses were never able to investigate it further. They learned about its contents from a neighborhood child who was small enough to crawl through the passageway. Apparently the Petersons had used it for a storage room.

The other room, in the turret, was a different matter. The Andrews family found it by accident when they noticed a removable panel at the rear of one of the third-floor closets. Opening it, they found a crawl space some three feet wide, leading out into the eaves. At first they assumed it was a shaft for ventilation . . . but then Lee became curious. She recruited her boyfriend, Neil Seamans, and asked him to find out where the crawl space led.

Armed with a flashlight, Neil pulled himself through the hole. It was a tight fit for a six-foot-three, 225-pound man, but somehow he wormed his way along the eaves, down the length of the house . . . and discovered an opening into the attic of the turret. It was too small for him to get through, although it might have accommodated an average-size person. Neil stuck his head and one shoulder through the hole and aimed his flashlight into the interior of the attic.

The hidden room was small, perhaps five feet in diameter, and its ceiling was high enough for a man to stand upright. The whole interior—walls, ceiling, and floor—was painted black. High up on one wall was a grayish-white painting of a horned animal's head—the creature reminded Neil of a ram. He shuddered, glanced down, and saw another design, this one on the floor, also grayish-white but star-shaped. In the center of it lay an old bundle of cloth. By stretching, Neil managed to snag it with his fingertips and drag it into the eaves. There he examined the bundle by flashlight. It held a badly rusted nickel-plated firearm known around the turn of the century as a "whore-gun." The cloth wrapped around it resembled a baby's dress; by the way it had rusted to the gun, it seemed that both items had been wet at the time of the wrapping.

A ram's head, a pentagram, a baby's dress, and a gun—all hidden in a dead-black secret room in the turret! Might there really be truth to the old "witch's-house" story? Neil didn't know and wasn't sure he wanted to find out. Tucking the bundle into his pocket, he turned and worked his way carefully back down the eaves. The Andrews family was intrigued when he gave them the cloth and gun, but no one went back to investigate further.

The other rooms in the house had some interesting quirks of their own. Family members often heard voices coming from the downstairs bathroom, for example, night and day. Usually several voices were involved, both male and female, in what sounded like a lively discussion. But they weren't speaking English. Lee thought it might be German or a Slavic language, but never found anyone who could understand it. She found it disconcerting to undress in there, with an invisible crowd chatting merrily around her.

Still, the voices didn't stop Eva from taking in roomers. Some people, she reasoned, might enjoy a few ghosts; besides, the family needed the money. A colorful ad was placed in the local paper, and shortly thereafter the first tenants arrived. They were artists for the most part, creative and, not infrequently, eccentric people. The old house seemed to suit them. Unfortunately, some of them didn't seem to suit the house. . . .

The first hint of trouble came when one gentleman roomer—who had admittedly been known to drink—came racing ashen-faced downstairs, screaming that he couldn't stay in the house any longer.

"There's a glowing ball of blue light in my room!" he informed his landlady. "And it follows me around!"

Eva Andrews smiled indulgently, assuming that the "ball" had rolled out of a bottle. Since the man was so upset, she let him move out without discussion. No more was said of the sighting, until a couple of weeks later, when Mrs. Andrews met the mist-ball herself.

She was down on hands and knees, stripping wax off the upstairs hall floor, when she suddenly glanced up and saw a glowing ball of blue mist drifting toward her. Irritated more than scared, she raced downstairs, grabbed a broom, and returned, prepared for battle. But the ball was gone. Eva checked the nearby rooms; then, finding no trace of her "visitor," she leaned the broom against the wall and went back to stripping wax.

A few minutes later she realized she was being watched. She turned—and saw the mist-ball hovering directly behind her. Snatching up the broom, she swatted at it. The ball promptly disappeared and never bothered her again.

It did, however, follow a lot of other people around—among them Lee, her sister Petra, and a number of the roomers. And on at least one occasion it showed up in a photograph, although no one had seen it when the picture was taken.

Another roomer, a German World War II veteran who had served under the Nazis, lived in the second-floor turret room, and on four separate occasions was charged with exposing himself from his window to young girls walking by in the street below. The police investigation turned up some interesting facts. For one thing, the roomer wasn't home when the offending incidents occurred. For another, the description of the man—stocky, middle-aged, with dark hair—didn't fit the former sailor, or anyone else living in the house at the time. It *did*, however, fit the late Mr. Peterson. The Andrews family began to wonder about the possibility of a ghost. Peterson, they remembered, had been Danish by birth and had served with the Allies. Perhaps he resented an ex-Nazi in his house and wanted to cause him trouble.

The more the Andrews family considered it, the more certain they became that Mr. Peterson's ghost was inhabiting the house. Peterson had died very suddenly—so suddenly that he might not realize he was dead. And the house was full of his things: navy uniforms, tools, some paintings he'd done, even his books with his name written on them. It must be terribly confusing for him to return home, only to find his house inhabited by strangers!

As the months went by, the ghost seemed to learn new tricks. Very often—at least a few times a week—a crash would be heard from the kitchen, as if someone had dropped a book flat on its side from a great height. This usually happened during fireside conversations, as if the ghost was expressing his agreement with some statement. The family's reaction was lighthearted; they would all point to the kitchen, saying, "That must be the truth!"

The ghost took on the behavior of a poltergeist. Objects began to travel around the house; the most notorious was a pewter candy dish formerly belonging to Mrs. Peterson, left behind when she moved. It was about five inches in diameter and usually sat on the mantelpiece in the living room, filled with wax fruit. However, it turned up in some very odd places—the upstairs broom closet, for example—locked doors notwithstanding. The Andrewses assumed someone was moving it as a prank... until the great blackout of 1965.

Like the rest of the northeastern United States and Canada, Toronto found itself plunged into chaos and darkness. Understandably nervous, the Andrews family and their roomers congregated in the living room to pass the time by candlelight. By three A.M. they were telling ghost stories. Abruptly the pewter dish—which had been sitting on the coffee table—rose up spontaneously, whizzed into the kitchen, and bounced off the refrigerator with a resounding *clang*! Nobody had touched it or been anywhere near it.

The family and their tenants stared at each other, incredulous. They had all seen the dish fly, but they weren't sure they believed it. Finally Lee went out to the kitchen and picked it up off the floor. There was a deep dent in one side of the dish and another in the refrigerator. She brought it back into the living room and replaced it on the table. The next day Eva put the pewter dish in the bottom of a clothes box in her closet and locked the door. The dish appeared on the third floor two weeks later.

Even the animals of the household were affected by the hauntings. Lee's cat would often arch her back and hiss at one particular spot in the upstairs hallway. Whenever Lee went to investigate, she felt a strange chill in the area. And the family dog, a friendly little terrier, flatly refused to go into the basement. If someone tried to drag him bodily down the stairs, he would resist frantically, whining and bristling in terror.

One roomer managed to make friends with the ghost. Jack Sturgeon was a tall, cadaverous fellow in his mid-fifties, with dark salt-and-pepper hair and intense jet-black eyes. He lived at the Peterson mansion off and on for four years, from 1965 to 1969; and, like most of the roomers, he was a trifle eccentric. A complete vegetarian, he ate applesauce with his mashed potatoes, claimed that Sturgeon was his Indian name (although he was obviously Anglo-Saxon), and always paid his room rent in fifty-cent pieces. He also tended to stretch the truth on occasion. However, in addition to all his other quirks, he did have a rapport with the ghost.

In the basement was a workbench where Eva and the roomers often set up their easels. Eva was an enthusiastic artist who often talked her boarders into joining her in an impromptu painting lesson. Eva reported that after being totally engrossed in her work for some time, she would suddenly become distracted, feeling that she was intruding on someone's privacy. So strong was this sensation that she would throw down her brush and scramble for the stairs. The other artists who painted down there had similar experiences . . . all but Jack, who told the household that he spoke to the spirit and knew who it had been.

One night, by the fire in the big living room, Jack told them this story:

"There are Drugeon forces about—spirits who roam the earth and obtain their energy from the life-giving essence of sleeping humans."

The luckless group of cynics looked skeptically at him. All their lives were well-grounded in the physical world. Lee was a nursing student; her mother was a telephone operator; and the roomers ran the gamut from university students to an electrical engineer, an accountant, a teacher, and a prostitute. When they saw that Jack was serious, muffled snickers ensued.

But the indomitable Sturgeon was not put off by their mockery. "I'm not afraid of the soul who haunts these rooms," he went on. "I have made contact with him. He does not know why all these people are in his house; he cannot find his wife, and worries about her because she has only one good eye and can't do for herself. He does not realize that he has passed over to the next place; he died so quickly in the crash. He has simply come home to look for his wife."

Eva Andrews was startled. Most of what Jack had just told them could have been picked up from ghost stories and neighborhood gossip, *except the fact that Mrs. Peterson was missing an eye!* Only Eva knew that; Mrs. Peterson had told her, in strict confidence, about the accident in which she'd lost the use of it. She'd been driving up Hamilton Mountain when a passing motorist had thrown a pop bottle from his vehicle; it had struck her in the face, damaging one eye permanently. She was sensitive about it—most of the neighbors didn't know. How, then, had Jack found out?

Jack was now a confidant of the ghostly Mr. Peterson, and the house reacted to Jack in special ways. Whenever he roomed there, the Andrewses would be warned of his homecoming by pictures falling off the walls. It was the only time they fell. The omen was quite reliable; Lee would shout, "Jack's coming, the blue nude just fell off the wall!" And five minutes later, in he'd stroll, grinning broadly.

The ghost was musical and would often perform for an audience. He particularly enjoyed playing the piano. In early 1967, when a reporter from the Montreal *Bell News* came to interview Eva about her haunted house, Peterson played a single clear chord on the piano, right in front of her. (The reporter later said her hands shook and her hair stood on end.) And at three o'clock every morning, he would strum Lee's cello, one string at a time, in sequence, for fifteen minutes—G-D-A, G-D-A, over and over—regardless of who might be listening. Since the cello was kept in the downstairs turret room beside the piano, and since both were right next to Eva Andrews' bedroom door, it woke her every night. If anyone physically touched the cello strings during Peterson's performance, the strumming would stop ... only to resume the next night.

The cello-strumming was not limited to the early-morning hours. One evening Lee and a guest were treated to a performance. Doug Southam was a six-foot-six-inch California blacksmith who followed the racing circuit. He had fought in Korea and wasn't afraid of anything, least of all ghosts. It took Peterson to make a believer of him.

About nine o'clock one evening, Doug and Lee were sitting together in the kitchen, drinking tea. The door to the living room was open and they could see the whole length of the house, past the piano to the turret where Lee's cello stood against the wall. Dandy, the terrier, was lying curled up by the bookcase just inside the dining-room door. Suddenly the top three strings of the cello sounded—G, D, and finally A—as if some unseen hand were strumming the instrument. Lee looked at Doug; Doug looked at Lee; the dog looked at the cello. For a moment silence reigned.

Then Doug said with a shrug, "It's just the wind or something." Lee knew he was wrong, but didn't bother to argue.

Five minutes later the scene repeated itself. The top three cello strings sounded, G-D-A. Again Doug shrugged it off, and again Lee remained silent, but the terrier looked nervously at the cello and whined.

Another five minutes passed—then the same thing again. As the strings sounded, the dog climbed to his feet with a look of disgust, padded into the kitchen, and began scratching at the door. Doug looked from him to the cello, then got up.

"I don't know what this is," he told Lee uneasily, "but I'm going to follow that dog's lead and get the hell out of here!"

Lee nodded agreement, and both man and dog retreated. The cello stopped playing as soon as they left.

The strumming wasn't string slippage; Lee had checked that out for herself. Like all stringed instruments, cellos are very sensitive to weather changes, and string slippage is common, but she had learned to recognize that by its characteristic "pinging" sound. Peterson's strumming sounded different. Furthermore, after several ghostly "concerts" Lee had tried to retune the instrument (if the strings had slipped, it would have been out of tune), and every time, she had found herself unable to improve on the cello as it stood. This was doubly surprising because Lee had been gifted with "perfect pitch" and would normally have made some adjustment to any instrument that had stood for a while without being played.

Inevitably Lee's classmates heard about the resident ghost. Intrigued by the occult but knowing nothing about ghosts, they decided to conduct their own séance. One day, Lee and three of her friends (two boys and a girl) cut their afternoon classes and headed down to the basement, armed with a plaster skull, a Ouija board, and the "flying" pewter dish. Their plan was to contact the ghost—Peterson, or whoever it was—and tell him that he was dead and should go somewhere else. Unfortunately, things turned out a little differently than they expected.

The four intrepid young ghost-hunters settled themselves around a small round table with the Ouija board in the middle. They were less than a dozen feet from the laundry-room door (the laundry room had always been a favorite haunt of the ghost) and commanded a view of the entire basement. Presumably because she lived there, Lee was selected as the medium. No one was aware at the time—not even Lee herself—that she was psychic (she has since demon-

strated strong abilities in both palmistry and telepathy).
The basement was pitch dark. Two candles were lit: one
on top of the plaster skull, the other in a tall candle-
stick. The four ghost-hunters each placed a finger on
the Ouija-board pointer (they were using the levitating
pewter dish!) and began asking questions. The first
question was, "Is there a spirit present?"

The pointer whizzed over to "Yes."

Immediately all four students accused each other
of moving the pointer. It took a few moments to estab-
lish that no one had moved it. Then they began to
argue about what they should ask the ghost. The question they finally decided on was, "What is your name?"

Slowly the pointer moved from letter to letter,
spelling out "P-e-d-e-r-s-e-n."

The teenagers were startled. Not only had the
ghost just identified itself as the former owner of the
house, but it had spelled its surname in the Danish
fashion, using a D and an E instead of a T and an O—
presumably the original version. Everyone else in the
neighborhood, including Mr. Peterson himself before
his death, had used the English spelling. There was no
chance now that any of the students could be manipu-
lating the Ouija board.

The next question was, "Why are you here?"
Quickly the pointer spelled out "H-o-m-e."

Growing bolder, the students pressed on. "Where
are you?"

Then the Ouija-board ghost spelled "D-a-r-k."

The teenagers were getting nervous. Lee suggested that they stop using the Ouija board and get the
séance going in earnest. They all joined hands, and after
some preliminary giggling and pinching, began to
concentrate.

Lee intoned: "Pedersen, if you are here, make
your presence known." The others took up the chant.

In the flickering candlelight, the atmosphere in the room began to change subtly. The teenagers continued to chant: "Pedersen, if you are here, make your presence known. . . ."

Lee felt herself sliding into a trance. Although she has since become highly proficient at trancing, she was more than a little frightened by this, her first time. Her consciousness drew inward; she found herself hanging suspended in darkness, alone, surrounded by a faint blue glow. The other teenagers had disappeared from her awareness, although she could still hear their voices chanting. Involuntarily she shivered . . . and heard the scrape of leather-soled shoes on concrete. Walking. Toward her.

The footsteps were coming from the laundry room. All four froze, scared silly, unable to let go of each other. Lee, still in a trance, broke the circle and extended her hand toward the laundry-room door.

"If you are there," she whispered, "let us know. Touch us."

The door of the laundry room scraped grindingly inward, opening about four inches.

By now the other students were terrified, too frightened to move. Lee kept chanting, "Touch us. Touch us." And an icy cold electric force took hold of her arm. Her left hand was still part of the circle, joined in a chain to the hands of the others. The force raced through her, into the other three, locking them together and freezing them in place. Before, they had simply been too frightened to break free of each other. Now they literally were unable to. The other three began screaming, "I can't let go!" Lee was the only calm one . . . because she was still in a trance.

A blue glow began seeping out from behind the laundry-room door. The force had hold of all of them. Inexorably, Lee felt herself being dragged toward the laundry room, pulling her companions along. The others resisted mightily, but were unable to hold her back. She was halfway to the laundry room when another girl let out a bloodcurdling scream of operatic proportions. The cry startled Lee out of her trance; she roused, and the spell was broken. All four teenagers let go and bolted like scared rabbits for the staircase. That was the last time anyone in the house ever attempted to contact the ghost.

The strange hauntings continued: electric lights dimmed and brightened unaccountably, one room at a time. Fireplace pokers went flying around the living room. In late 1973 the Andrews family decided they'd had enough and sold the house to a bright-eyed young couple, newly married. No mention was made of the ghost, for obvious reasons. Not only might the couple not believe them, but if they did, they might not buy the house. The Andrews family held their breath and moved out of Toronto.

But they stayed in touch with their old neighbors, curious about what Mr. Peterson might do to the poor young couple. Time went by and they never heard a word. The new owners still live in the mansion and the house has never been sold again. Perhaps they find the idea of a poltergeist entertaining, or perhaps Mr. Peterson has moved on to another strange old house. . . .

ABOUT THE AUTHOR

SHARON JARVIS has been a reporter, a teacher, and a tracer of missing persons. For the last twenty years she has been involved in book publishing, primarily as an editor specializing in science fiction, fantasy, horror, and the occult. Currently she is a literary agent, operating out of a turn-of-the-century house on Staten Island, which friends swear must be haunted. Her companions are a cat and two dogs, one of whom is aptly nicknamed "Monster."

DON'T MISS
THESE CURRENT
Bantam Bestsellers

☐	27814	**THIS FAR FROM PARADISE** Philip Shelby	$4.95
☐	27811	**DOCTORS** Erich Segal	$5.95
☐	28179	**TREVAYNE** Robert Ludlum	$5.95
☐	27807	**PARTNERS** John Martel	$4.95
☐	28058	**EVA LUNA** Isabel Allende	$4.95
☐	27597	**THE BONFIRE OF THE VANITIES** Tom Wolfe	$5.95
☐	27456	**TIME AND TIDE** Thomas Fleming	$4.95
☐	27510	**THE BUTCHER'S THEATER** Jonathan Kellerman	$4.95
☐	27800	**THE ICARUS AGENDA** Robert Ludlum	$5.95
☐	27891	**PEOPLE LIKE US** Dominick Dunne	$4.95
☐	27953	**TO BE THE BEST** Barbara Taylor Bradford	$5.95
☐	26554	**HOLD THE DREAM** Barbara Taylor Bradford	$5.95
☐	26253	**VOICE OF THE HEART** Barbara Taylor Bradford	$5.95
☐	26888	**THE PRINCE OF TIDES** Pat Conroy	$4.95
☐	26892	**THE GREAT SANTINI** Pat Conroy	$4.95
☐	26574	**SACRED SINS** Nora Roberts	$3.95
☐	27018	**DESTINY** Sally Beauman	$4.95

Buy them at your local bookstore or use this page to order.

Special Offer
Buy a Bantam Book
for only 50¢.

Now you can have Bantam's catalog filled with hundreds of titles plus take advantage of our unique and exciting bonus book offer. A special offer which gives you the opportunity to purchase a Bantam book for only 50¢. Here's how!

By ordering any five books at the regular price per order, you can also choose any other single book listed (up to a $5.95 value) for just 50¢. Some restrictions do apply, but for further details why not send for Bantam's catalog of titles today!

Just send us your name and address and we will send you a catalog!

BANTAM BOOKS, INC.
P.O. Box 1006, South Holland, Ill. 60473

Mr./Mrs./Ms. _____
(please print)

Address _____

City _____ State _____ Zip _____

FC(A)-11/89

Please allow four to six weeks for delivery.

EXPLORE THE SPIRITUAL WORLD WITH SHIRLEY MacLAINE AND JESS STEARN

Check to see which of these fine titles are missing from your bookshelf:

Titles by Jess Stearn:

☐	26085	EDGAR CAYCE: SLEEPING PROPHET	$4.50
☐	25150	SOULMATES	$3.95
☐	26057	YOGA, YOUTH, AND REINCARNATION	$3.95

Titles by Shirley MacLaine:

☐	27557	DANCING IN THE LIGHT	$4.95
☐	27370	OUT ON A LIMB	$4.95
☐	27438	"DON'T FALL OFF THE MOUNTAIN"	$4.95
☐	26173	YOU CAN GET THERE FROM HERE	$4.95
☐	27299	IT'S ALL IN THE PLAYING	$4.95
☐	05367	GOING WITHIN	$18.95

Look for them in your bookstore or use the coupon below:

Bantam Books, Dept. PW4, 414 East Golf Road, Des Plaines, IL 60016

Please send me the items I have checked above. I am enclosing $_____ (please add $2.00 to cover postage and handling). Send check or money order, no cash or C.O.D.s please.

Mr/Ms _____

Address _____

City/State_____ Zip _____

PW4–11/89

Please allow four to six weeks for delivery.
Prices and availability subject to change without notice.